AMERICAN
LEGAL AND
CONSTITUTIONAL
        HISTORY ★ A Garland
                Series of
                Outstanding
                Dissertations

Edited by
    HAROLD HYMAN
    William P. Hobby Professor of History,
    Rice University

    STUART BRUCHEY
    Allan Nevins Professor of American
    Economic History, Columbia University

WOMEN VOTE
IN THE WEST ★ The Woman
Suffrage Movement
1869–1896

Beverly Beeton

Garland Publishing, Inc.
New York & London ★ 1986

Library of Congress Cataloging-in-Publication Data

Beeton, Beverly.
  Women vote in the West.

  (American legal and constitutional history)
  Bibliography: p.
    1. Women—Suffrage—West (U.S.)—History—19th
century.   2. West (U.S.)—Politics and government.
I. Title. II. Series.
JK1896.B44   1986   324.6′23′0978   86-4716
ISBN 0-8240-8251-6

All volumes in this series are printed on acid-free,
250-year-life paper.

Printed in the United States of America

Women Vote in the West:
The Woman Suffrage Movement, 1869-1896

Beverly Beeton

CONTENTS

PREFACE

As the nation began to reorder daily life after the Civil War, the pioneer suffragists, who had agitated for the vote for women in the decades before the conflict between the North and South, resumed their demand for equality for women and freedmen. When the Republican party and some former abolitionists informed the women that it was "the Negro's hour" and endorsed the Fourteenth and Fifteenth amendments which for the first time inserted the word "male" into the Constitution, Elizabeth Cady Stanton and Susan B. Anthony led a group of women out of the American Equal Rights Association and formed the National Woman Suffrage Association to campaign expressly for woman suffrage. Once the rights of black men seemed to be guaranteed by the Constitution, the more moderate woman suffragists rallied around Lucy Stone and her husband, Henry B. Blackwell, to establish the American Woman Suffrage Association.

While these two suffrage factions were centered in upstate New York and in Boston, legislation enfranchising women was first enacted in the Rocky Mountain region of the American West. The purpose of this study is to examine why woman suffrage was achieved during the period 1869 to 1896 in the area which today comprises Wyoming, Utah, Colorado, and Idaho. Of particular concern is the impact of Western suffrage on the national political scene and on the struggle for full enfranchisement of women which culminated in 1920 with the ratification of the Nineteenth Amendment. Although the text surveys the effort to gain suffrage in the West, the primary focus is on the four states where women were enfranchised in the nineteenth century—Wyoming, Utah, Colorado and Idaho.

In December of 1869 the Democratic-led territorial legislature of Wyoming, seeing female suffrage as a means to advertise the region and to have the additional satisfaction of embarrassing the puritanical Republican governor, extended the franchise to Wyoming women. Two months later in February of 1870, the Mormon-dominated Utah territorial legislature voted in the affirmative on a woman suffrage measure. Here, the principal motives were to counter accusations that Mormon women were downtrodden, ignorant slaves of the male hierarchy, to recruit the national suffrage organization to lobby against antipolygamy legislation pending in Congress, and to promote Utah's bid for statehood. But in both Utah and Wyoming the franchise was restricted by the territorial status of these two areas since citizens of territories are not allowed to vote in gubernatorial or presidential elections. Moreover, in 1887, with the passage of the Edmunds-Tucker Act designed to eliminate plural marriage as practiced by the Mormons, the United States Congress disfranchised the women of Utah Territory.

Later, in 1890 when Wyoming joined the union, it reaffirmed its two decades of experience with woman suffrage by adopting a constitution which carried a clause including women in the elective process; thus it became the first state, except New Jersey which had briefly permitted some women to vote at the end of the eighteenth century, to allow its adult female citizens to participate in all political elections.

Despite suffragists' petitions and territorial governors' requests for a woman suffrage bill, from 1869 to 1876 the Colorado territorial legislature was unwilling to extend political privileges to women. Even in 1876, when Colorado joined the union as the Centennial State, its constitution limited women's political participation to school district elections; moreover, in the next seventeen years repeated attempts to extend women full electoral privileges met with failure. It was not until 1893 that a Populist-supported woman suffrage referendum was approved. Thus, Colorado became the second state to allow its women to vote.

Following the Wyoming precedent, Utah joined the union in 1896 with a constitution reinstating woman suffrage. The same year, Idaho amended its constitution to allow women access to the ballot. In 1896 women were allowed full voting rights in these four Rocky Mountain states, but it would be fourteen years before any other states would extend such privileges to their female citizens and twenty-four years before women's right to the ballot would be recognized by an amendment to the federal constitution.

Why did women first realize the goal of the elective franchise in the nineteenth century American West? First, female suffrage was seen as a means to advertise a region in an effort to improve the image of a particular society or to attract investors and settlers. Secondly, it was often proposed as a political hoax to embarrass the opposition or was undertaken as an effort by a political faction to recruit women to its cause so that it could gain or hold political supremacy. Thirdly, the move for woman suffrage drew support from the reaction to the enfrachisement of black men in the Reconstruction Era. Fourthly, territorial residents saw that it could be used to recruit Eastern support in their campaigns for statehood. Finally, it seemed to be a safe place to experiment with woman suffrage, and there was little organized opposition to women voting in these areas.

In the West the vote was generally viewed as a privilege bestowed by the governing body, not an inherent right. More often than not, Western women and the Eastern suffrage movement were used by those in power to achieve other goals; and women were granted the ballot at a specific time, not simply for the liberal principles lauded by the Eastern movement, but for more pragmatic purposes, usually political. In short, women were enfranchised in the nineteenth century American West as a matter of expediency, not ideology.

The bibliographical notes at the back of this book cite the major sources used in this study and note the archives and libraries holding the most important materials for a study of suffrage in the West. I am indebted to numerous individuals and institutions for making this study possible. With gratitude I acknowledge the advice and sympathetic support provided by friends and colleagues, especially Philip C. Sturges of the Department of History at the University of Utah for his understanding encouragement and thoughtful counsel.

Beverly Beeton
University of Alaska-Juneau
August 1985

INTRODUCTION

By definition universal suffrage has traditionally excluded women. In modern history those who have advocated universal suffrage—Levellers, Chartists, and Jacksonians—have all sought the vote for adult, usually white, men.

Women were defined as dependent beings incapable of independent decisions in political matters. This concept of dependence was also expressed in the argument that women were represented politically by their men. In keeping with Blackstone's statement of the common law, upon marriage a woman's legal existence was suspended, or, as he phrased it, incorporated in that of her husband, and she was said to be in a state of coverture. The indivisibility of sovereignty as it related to the family, as well as to government, was a popular idea in the eighteenth century Anglo-American world. In short, upon marriage man and woman become one, and the one was the husband. This concept of household suffrage persisted through most of the nineteenth century. In some respects, the legal status of single and widowed women was better than that of married women; yet they were not considered whole people with unqualified political or property rights.

It was not until mid-nineteenth century that sustained efforts began to redefine universal suffrage to include women. Harriet Taylor, in her 1851 article on the enfranchisement of women, and John Stuart Mill, in his essay on the subjection of women and in his legislative fights in Parliament, most forcefully articulated the political rights of women to a wide audience in England. In 1867, when Disraeli's conservatives were pushing an electoral reform bill, Mill made an unsuccessful bid to extend the franchise to women.

As Mill's rhetoric demonstrates, the struggle for female enfranchisement has been in the mainline liberal tradition. Woman suffrage rhetoric, goals, assumptions, and methods have largely been drawn from the liberal credo. This ideological base was British in origin, but the early campaign for women's political power centered in the United States.

In this country the organized efforts demanding enfranchisement of women date from the 1840's. Just two decades earlier property qualifications had been swept away, and suffrage rights had been extended to most adult, white, male citizens. But it was not until women became involved in the abolition of slavery and other reform movements in the 1840's that the campaign was begun to attack the sexual barricade to political participation. Using rhetoric from the liberal-whig catechism and borrowing directly from the Declaration of Independence, the pioneer woman suffragists, who gathered at Seneca Falls, New York in 1848, argued that the franchise was a natural, inalienable, inherent right. Defining women as people for the purpose of political rights, they initiated the campaign to secure the ballot.

During the decade prior to the Civil War, the Seneca Falls advocates expanded their activities into the surrounding states, holding meetings and gaining support for their ideas in Massachusetts, Ohio, and Pennsylvania. In these years the women's rights movement was closely tied with the abolition movement; abolition leaders, both men and women, generally supported women's rights and spoke at suffrage conventions. Most suffrage activities were suspended during the Civil War as abolitionists and women's rights workers threw themselves into the war effort, but at the close of the war some of the reformers, acting under the auspices of the American Equal Rights Association, resumed their demand for equal rights and the political franchise for women and freedmen.

While the Radical Republicans were formulating a proposed Fourteenth Amendment to the Constitution to guarantee freedmen political power, the Kansas legislature submitted two amendments to that state's constitution: one proposition was black enfranchisement, the other female enfranchisement. Initially, the prospects for suffrage were hopeful because Kansas had shown evidence of moving towards a broadening of the electorate by including school suffrage for women in its 1861 constitution. At the request of the Kansas Republican Senators, suffrage speakers were sent west to canvass the area and conduct an equal rights convention. Lucy Stone and her husband Henry B. Blackwell, representing the American Equal Rights Association, campaigned for a month in Kansas and returned east with optimistic reports that the Republicans had started an irreversible movement for equal rights for women and black men.

This optimism, however, was premature. As the summer wore on and the campaign intensified, the editors of the national and local Republican and reform newspapers tended to support the idea of political privileges for black men but generally neglected comment on the subject of the ballot for women. By witholding their endorsements of woman suffrage, the Kansas Republican party and the national reform newspapers weakened the cause. However, it was the American Equal Rights Association on Suffrage, chaired by Horace Greeley, which delivered the fatal blow when it reported that the members of the committee felt the extension of the elective franchise to women would be too revolutionary and sweeping for public acceptance. Bolstered by such waivering on the part of the foremost national organization in favor of equality for women, skeptical Republicans in Kansas publicly announced their unwillingness to support the woman suffrage referendum. Consequently, antifeminist sentiments became acceptable. Even the Kansas Republican Central Committee spokesmen urged party faithful not to vote for woman suffrage and simultaneously threw party strength behind what they referred to as the great question of manhood suffrage. In short, the party decided to make a push for the enfranchisement of black men while ignoring political rights for women.

When Susan B. Anthony and Elizabeth Cady Stanton arrived in Kansas late in the summer of 1867, they found that the mood was turning more and more against women. In spite of the fact that letters from John Stuart Mill and copies of his speeches were circulated and that reprints of Harriet Taylor's 1851 article were made available, few citizens seemed willing to endorse woman suffrage.

Without the official support of the Republican party or the wholehearted backing of the American Equal Rights Association, Stanton and Anthony pessimistically faced the last month of the campaign. At this point, George Francis Train, an avid Democrat and friend of unconventional people and radical movements, joined the camp of woman suffrage supporters. Having made a fortune as a railroad promoter and financier, Train loaned money and donated his personal time to the cause. As the sunflowers blossomed, George Francis Train and Susan B. Anthony carried the campaign from one Kansas town to the next delivering speeches in favor of woman suffrage. Harassed and criticized by abolitionists and Republicans for their alliances with Train, Stanton and Anthony replied, "Your test of faithfulness is the Negro, ours is the woman."

As Stanton, Anthony, and Train continued the campaign, national reform newspapers belatedly tried to convince Kansas Republicans that the question was really one of universal suffrage—the vote for both women and black men. But they had been silent on the subject of woman suffrage too long. Most Kansas Republicans seemed convinced that the vote for black men was the cause and that if identified with woman suffrage it would be defeated. At this point even Horace Greeley begrudgingly acknowledged in his New York *Tribune* that though he regarded female suffrage with distrust, he was quite willing to see it pioneered in Kansas. When the votes were tallied, however, both propositions failed.

Neither women nor black men gained the political franchise in this vigorous Kansas campaign in 1867. Nonetheless, as a result of this effort the woman suffrage movement began to assume the form that it would take for the next thirty years. Aggressive suffragists like Stanton and Anthony felt betrayed by equal rights reformers like Horace Greeley, Wendell Phillips, George T. Curtis, and Theodore Tilton with whom they had worked for years before and during the Civil War. In the Kansas fight these men had used their influence to support suffrage for black males but had ignored or only mildly supported woman suffrage. As Stanton analyzed it: "The philosophy of their indifference we thoroughly comprehended for the first time and saw as never before, that only from woman's standpoint could the battle be successfully fought, and victory secured."[1] At this point, these women abandoned their long reliance on male reformers and moved in the direction of a genuine women's movement.

Disillusioned by the lack of support from the Equal Rights Association but still optimistic about the cause of woman suffrage, Stanton and Anthony, financed and accompanied by George Francis Train, made their return trip to the East a speaking tour. When the three arrived in New York, Train put up enough money to launch a woman suffrage paper. Christened the *Revolution*, the new weekly first appeared in January 1868, with Anthony as publisher and Stanton as editor. Radical by the standards of the day, the *Revolution* vigorously opposed the Fourteenth and Fifteenth amendments, advocating instead suffrage for the educated, irrespective of sex or color.

During the Kansas campaign Hamilton Willcox, a representative of the New York Universal Franchise Association, had proposed that women in all the territories be enfranchised, and the New York *Times* had publicized this scheme for testing woman suffrage. In 1868-1869, when the Radical Republicans were trying to persuade Congress to go beyond the already ratified Fourteenth Amendment and guarantee freedmen's right to vote, similar measures were introduced attempting to provide women with access to the ballot. But there was little support in Congress for the suggestion that the proposed Fifteenth Amendment include a prohibition against denying or abridging citizens' right to vote on the basis of sex, and even less enthusiasm for a separate amendment, recommended by Kansas Senator Samuel C. Pomeroy, specifically enfranchising women.

Willcox's scheme for testing woman suffrage, given legislative form by the Indiana Republican congressman George Washington Julian, intrigued a few congressmen. Experimenting with woman suffrage in the territories was appealing to some congressmen because it appeared to be safe. Neither the political stability of the established states nor the national political scene would be seriously altered because territorial voters could not vote for their own governors or for the President. Moreover, since Congress controlled the territories, the experiment could easily be halted if it seemed to go awry. It appeared that the impact women would have on politics and the possible defeminizing impact that politics would have on women could be safely tested in the territories. Two side effects which Willcox and others predicted were: the movement of "surplus women" from the East to the West and the elimination of the Mormon men's practice of marrying multiple wives.

Population redistribution or Mormon plural marriage were not the primary concerns of women who advocated equal rights; they insisted women had inherent natural rights. When equal rights suffragists convened in Washington, D.C., in January, 1869, to lobby for federal legislation enfranchising women, Elizabeth Cady Stanton called for the passage of a constitutional amendment guaranteeing women's political rights as the proposed Fifteenth Amendment did for freedmen. Universal Franchise Association representatives testified before the House Committee on Territories in favor of Julian's bill to enfranchise women in the territories, while the vice president of the District of Columbia branch of the association, Belva McNall Lockwood, lobbied for the passage of this legislation.

Yet, by spring it was apparent that while the idea that suffrage based on citizenship without regard to race or color was gaining acceptance, the barrier of sex was still strong. The idea of a constitutional amendment for woman suffrage was being completely ignored and the proposal to test the concept in the territories now seemed to have small chance of success. As Julian's bill now read, it was limited to Utah Territory where the concern was with using woman suffrage as a means to eradicate Mormon polygamy which, along with slavery, was referred to as a "relic of barbarism."

Many woman suffragists were convinced, and consequently angry, that their abolitionist and Republican allies were insisting it was "the Negro's hour." Thus, some suffragists felt betrayed, and as a consequence, this coupled with basic philosophical disagreements on goals and methods, supporters of equal suffrage split into two camps. The National Woman Suffrage Association, an aggressive all-woman organization, was formed under the leadership of Elizabeth Cady Stanton and Susan B. Anthony; the more moderate supporters of woman suffrage rallied to the banner of the American Woman Suffrage Association headed by Lucy Stone, Henry B. Blackwell, and Julia Ward Howe. While the National group demanded immediate woman suffrage, the American Association conceded that it was indeed "the Negro's hour"; thus they accepted deferred action on women's right to the ballot.

The New York-based Stanton-Anthony faction persisted in the fight for a national constitutional amendment fashioned after the Fifteenth; nonetheless, almost a decade would pass before such a proposal would again be introduced in Congress on the occasion of the centennial of the American Revolution, and not until 1920 would it finally be adopted. The Boston-based Stone faction was more traditional, insisting on a state's rights position with regard to woman suffrage. As this view was expressed in the *Woman's Journal*, the American association members believed each state constitution should be modified to allow for the enfranchisement of women. This schism on goals and methods would persist until 1890, when the two factions would be merged into the National American Woman Suffrage Association.

While the supporters of the American Equal Rights Association were aligning themselves into new woman suffrage organizations, and various proposals to test woman suffrage in the territories were being discussed in the national Congress, one after another, the territorial legislatures of Dakota, Wyoming, Utah, Colorado, New Mexico, and Idaho considered the feasibility of granting the ballot to women. When brought to a vote the idea was rejected everywhere except in Wyoming and Utah.

Notes

[1]Elizabeth Cady Stanton, Susan B. Anthony, Matilda J. Gage, and Ida H. Harper, *History of Woman Suffrage,* 6 vols. (originally published 1881-1922, reprint edition, New York: Arno, 1969), 2:267.

I. EQUALITY IN WYOMING

The philanthropic Territorial Legislature of Wyoming, fully appreciating 'Women's Rights' by understanding the many wrongs they were obliged to endure in all this great and otherwise freedom-loving land, were the first in this great interest to extend to women the elective franchise. The law here gives both sexes the same right as to voting; and that class of ladies who truly wish to enjoy such privileges, can very soon (with the present traveling facilities) not only see, but be landed in a short time safely in this promised land, to them, where they sit, if not under a fig tree under the lengthened shadows of the mountains, in the fullness of that great ballot power which makes and unmakes States and Empires.

George W. Pine
Beyond the West

True, the territorial legislature of Wyoming was the first such body in the nineteenth century to extend the elective franchise to women. But did the representatives of the newly organized territory act because they fully appreciated women's rights? The hope of advertising the existence of the territory, thereby promoting the immigration of people and capital, coupled with a desire to embarrass the governor were the most powerful factors in the legislators' decision to grant women of Wyoming[1] access to the political ballot in December of 1869. At that time the total population of Wyoming numbered less than 9,000 of which only about 1,200 were women of voting age.

Within nine months of the completion of the transcontinental railroad in 1869, the women of Wyoming were enfranchised. As George Pine noted, women seeking political authority now had a promised land, and the railroad provided an easy means to reach that supposed paradise on the crest of the continent. The completion of the railroad had linked Wyoming with the East, and many citizens of the newly organized territory were seeking a way to draw attention and hopefully attract settlers to the area. Woman suffrage seemed to be a powerful advertisement gimmick.

As has been noted, the idea of extending women the ballot in the sparsely populated Western territories was not totally new. As early as 1867, Hamilton Willcox of the Universal Franchise Association had raised the possibility of testing woman suffrage by enfranchising the women of the territories. This idea, popularized by the New York *Times*, had caught the attention of a congressman from Indiana, George Washington Julian, who in 1868 had introduced legislation in Congress designed to give the women of the territories the vote. When Willcox and other observers appeared before congressional committees in support of Julian's legislative propositions, their arguments favoring enfranchising women of Western territories hinged on the hope that the presence of political power might induce women to emigrate from what was considered by many to be the over-crowded East.[2]

Anna Elizabeth Dickenson

William H. Bright

Although many Wyoming residents were probably aware of the debate in Congress, within the territory, talk of enfranchising women was stimulated by speeches from the well-known lecturer and national suffrage leader, Anna Dickenson, who journeyed west on a speaking tour within six months of the completion of the railroad in 1869. Other support was raised by Redelia Bates, a woman suffrage lecturer from St. Louis, who spoke on the subject before Wyoming's first territorial leigislature.

One week after Redelia Bates' address, the president of Wyoming's legislative council, William H. Bright, gave notice that he would soon introduce a woman suffrage bill. He was encouraged by Edward M. Lee, an advocate of women's rights who had migrated from Connecticut to serve as secretary to the newly created territory. Bright, a native of Virginia who had served as postal agent in Salt Lake City and had moved to South Pass with the announcement of the gold discoveries, did introduce such a bill to enfranchise the women of Wyoming, employing the arguments most frequently used in the absence of direct pressure from women: to advertise the territory; to attract women to the territory where there were six men to every woman; to make women politically equal with black men; and most importantly to put Governor John A. Campbell on the spot by forcing him to sign or veto the bill—either action sure to produce protest. Non-smoking, non-drinking, Republican Campbell seemed too puritanical for the Democratic frontier legislators, and like most territorial governors, he was an Easterner, not of their choosing but rather a Presidential appointee.[3]

Both Edward M. Lee and William H. Bright philosophically supported the idea of allowing women to vote, but they also saw it as an effective means to call attention to the newly organized territory. Furthermore, by promoting his woman suffrage bill as a means to embarrass the governor, Bright was able to convince most of his fellow legislators to vote for the measure.[4]

The enfranchising bill was passed in the council without much difficulty, but the opposition in the house was effectively led by a South Pass City lawyer, Ben Sheeks, who succeeded in raising the age of qualification from eighteen to twenty-one. After nearly a month of consideration, in December of 1869, the council and the lower house passed the female suffrage act providing that every woman of the age of twenty-one residing in the territory could vote. In addition, this law affirmed women's right to hold office.

When the bill was transmitted to Governor John A. Campbell, a small delegation of women, led by a local suffrage advocate, Amelia Post, reportedly appeared at the governor's residence, making it clear they intended to stay there until the bill was signed into law.[5] Without hesitation or public discussion, and to the amazement of most legislators, Campbell quietly signed the act granting women of Wyoming the right to vote and to hold office.

Six months after passage of the woman suffrage law, Secretary Edward Lee, while serving as acting governor, took the advice of Associate Supreme Court Justice J. W. Kingman and appointed Caroline Neil and Esther Morris as Justices of the

Esther Morris

Governor John A. Campbell

Peace in Sweetwater county. When these two appointments were challenged in the courts, Morris was judged qualified and subsequently served in that capacity for eight and one-half months. Going even further, the territorial supreme court, which consisted of two well known advocates of women's rights John W. Kingman and J. H. Howe, handed down the decision that women had the right to sit on juries in Wyoming under the provisions of the existing territorial laws. Thus, in 1870 women of Wyoming were not only voting, but were sitting on juries and holding public office.

From the outset women's rights in Wyoming received the strong support of most of the appointed, usually Republican, officials of the territory. Of particular importance were Secretary Lee, Governor Campbell and Justices Kingman and Howe. Certainly Edward M. Lee was not a stranger to the idea of women voting. Two years before moving to Wyoming to assume the duties as secretary of the territory, Lee had sponsored an unsuccessful campaign in the Connecticut legislature to amend that state's constitution to allow for woman suffrage. Moreover, Hamilton Willcox reported that Lee had been in the national capital during the spring of 1869 when there was extensive discussion concerning the prospect of enfranchising women in the territories.[6]

The process whereby women in Wyoming were enfranchised in 1869 demonstrates the ease with which women in a territory could be granted the right to vote. The procedure was much less complicated than the process used by the states and did not require as much support. A total of only thirteen men in Wyoming's council and house voted for the measure, leaving six in opposition and one absent, and the bill became law upon endorsement by the governor. No constitutional amendment or submission to the electorate was necessary as would have been the case in a state. In short, a total of fourteen people acting in their official capacities brought the law into existence. Although some acted in accord with principles of justice, some considered it a joke, and some saw it as a way to embarrass a political opponent, most apparently seemed convinced that it would attract attention to their fledgling territory.

Reportedly, Eliza A. "Grandma" Swain, a seventy-five-year-old Quaker, was the first woman to cast her ballot in Laramie in the September 1870 election. One observer of the historic election day noted that women arrived at the polls and deposited "their votes with no more exposure to insult or injury than they would expect on visiting a grocery store or meat-market. Indeed," he observed, "they were much safer here, every man of their party was pledged to shield them, while every member of the other party feared the influence of any signs of disrespect."[7]

Once the votes were counted, it was apparent that the women had been instrumental in turning out the Democratic legislators who had voted to grant them suffrage. According to the local newspapers, the women had "worked actively for, and voted squarely the reform ticket, or in other words the straight Republican ticket."[8]

Immediately, some Eastern suffragists pointed to the example of Wyoming to

Women voting for the first time in Wyoming
September 6, 1870

Edward M. Lee

promote the cause in the East. Reporting that Wyoming's Chief Justice John H. Howe had expressed the belief that women would be able to bring about reforms, " 'which the unaided exertions of men had been incompetent to effect,' " Paulina W. Davis, speaking before the second decade commemoration of the women's rights movement in New York, speculated that:

> The question will therefore naturally suggest itself, if women in their new political capacity, are thus able to 'tone' the rude elements of Western civilization, what inconsistency is there in granting them like privileges in communities whose superior refinement is so much less likely to expose them to insult or mortification?[9]

When Susan B. Anthony reported the news of the enfranchising act in Wyoming at the National Woman Suffrage Association convention, she advised women "to emigrate to Wyoming and make a model State of it by sending a woman Senator to the National Capitol."[10] As for herself, she announced that she was going to remain at home and work for a federal constitutional amendment to enfranchise all women. There is little evidence that Eastern women heeded Anthony's advice to go west. The argument that the opportunity for political equality would cause women to move to the Western territories proved unsound. Nevertheless, the fact that Wyoming had enfranchised her women was repeatedly used to advertise the region and to counter its hell-on-wheels, mining town image.

On the other hand, while Eastern women did not migrate to Wyoming where they could exercise the political privilege, they did employ the example of Wyoming in attempts to persuade their own state legislatures to extend the privilege to them and to encourage the national Congress to pass an amendment to the Constitution enabling women to vote nationwide.

While women in Wyoming Territory were voting, Eastern suffragists were consolidating their new organizations. The National Woman Suffrage Association held its 1871 convention in Washington, D. C., where it lobbied congressmen for action on a national amendment for woman suffrage. Flanked by representatives of the suffrage association, Victoria Woodhull, free-love advocate, self-proclaimed candidate for the presidency of the United States, and co-editor with her sister, Tennessee C. Claflin of the radical *Woodhull and Claflin Weekly*, delivered a woman suffrage memorial to the Judiciary Committee of the House of Representatives. Although the memorial was supported by Representatives George Washington Julian of Indiana, Benjamin F. Butler of Massachusetts, and William Loughridge of Iowa, it was tabled. Nevertheless, the leaders of the suffrage organization were impressed with the notorious Victoria, and they invited her to address their convention. Belva Lockwood, Washington, D. C., advocate of universal suffrage, soon followed Woodhull's lead by memorializing Congress asking for suffrage for the women of the District of Columbia.

Within four months of this suffrage meeting, Elizabeth Cady Stanton was in the West sending Victoria Woodhull greetings from Wyoming, "the land of freedom." Stanton and Susan B. Anthony were in Laramie City delivering an address from the platform of the train which was taking them on to California on a Western lecture tour. During their brief stopover in Wyoming, the two suffragists were guests of women interested in political rights—Mrs. M. B. Arnold and Amelia B. Post. In addition, they made the acquaintance of a number of men who were key supporters of woman suffrage: Governor Campbell, Justices Howe and Kingman, and newspaper editor J. W. Hayford of the Laramie *Sentinel.* Seventy-five-year-old Eliza Swain was also on hand to meet the Eastern champions of women's rights.

On New Year's Eve, six months later, Anthony would be back in Laramie evaluating her suffrage activities for the year of 1871. She was on her way home to Rochester, then on to the National Woman Suffrage Association convention in Washington, D. C., after a half-year of lecturing in the West and on the Pacific Coast, when she was delayed in Wyoming due to deep snow. Thus, she was bringing a close to her diary for the year noting it was "a year *full* of close work"; she had traveled 13,000 miles and delivered over one hundred and seventy lectures only to find that she had a deficit of $2,271. Her lecture tour to California had not been the success she had expected. Hoping to duplicate Anna Dickenson's profitable 1869 lecture tour, Anthony had set out to see the wild West, to visit the regions where women voted, and to deliver lectures furthering the cause of woman suffrage while at the same time raising money to pay off the debts from the *Revolution.*[11] Shortly after her arrival in San Francisco, however, she had had her lectures cancelled and had incurred the wrath of the local press by visiting Laura D. Fair in jail where she was being held on a murder charge.[12] The whole affair became a full-blown furor when Anthony told an audience she was addressing on the power of the ballot that society was responsible for the fact that Laura Fair was charged with the murder of a man with whom she had an intimate relationship. Subsequently, Anthony found herself a lecturer without an audience.

So, while Stanton continued her lecture tour with the aid of California Suffragist Emily Pitt Stevens, Anthony had accepted an invitation to lecture in the Pacific Northwest with Abigail Scott Duniway, editor of the suffrage newspaper, the *New Northwest,* as her business manager. Here Anthony met with a generally friendly reception, and she had speaking engagements until she decided to return home around Christmas time.

Being snowbound in Wyoming was not as uncomfortable for Anthony as might be supposed, for she had accepted the invitation of the prosuffrage congressman from California, Aaron A. Sargent, to join him and his suffragist wife, Ellen on their trip east. Having caught up with the Sargents at Ogden, Utah, Anthony had joined them in their luxurious rail staterooms for the delay plagued trip across the Rocky Mountains.

While in Laramie, Anthony learned of the Wyoming territorial legislature's attempt to repeal the woman suffrage law; however, before she arrived in Cheyenne where she met with Governor Campbell, she had heard that he had vetoed the repeal act, saying, "No legislature has a right to disfranchise its own constituents."[13]

Amelia B. Post

In his veto message Governor Campbell had also assured the lawmakers that he felt it was simple justice to acknowledge that the women voters and jurors had conducted themselves with as much tact, sound judgment, and good sense as the men. Moreover, the governor reported, "The lessons of these two years' experience fully confirm all that has been claimed by the most ardent advocates."[14] Nevertheless, the Democrats in the legislature were determined. Led by the antisuffragist Ben Sheeks, now the Speaker of the House, the Democrats claimed the Republicans were harvesting the women's votes on election day and had, therefore, tried to repeal the act. Some of the opponents of woman suffrage felt so strongly about the subject that they offered Governor Campbell $2,000 to sign the repeal bill—an offer he refused.[15] When they tried to overturn the governor's veto, the members of the council and house divided along party lines thus defeating the effort, but only by one vote.

A representative of the American Woman Suffrage Association, Hannah M. Tracy Cutler, also toured the West in the summer of 1871. At a reception in her honor in Chicago, she reported that she had taken great pains while in Wyoming to assess the effect of the exercise of woman's suffrage, and she assured suffragists that the "disreputable women were very slightly represented at the polls, for the reason that they always concealed the name by which their parents or relatives could trace them out, and gave the names of the young men who shared their favors." As Hannah Cutler saw it, it was because the men did not want their names used at the polls by these women that "numerous elegant dresses and outfits were brought to bear, not to secure, but to keep away votes." Hannah Cutler's observations gave people east of the Mississippi River a colorful image of the Western territories where women voted. She embellished the story of women's power in Wyoming by saying, "In Laramie there were eleven women in the grand jury, and in two days twenty-eight dram shops had been closed up, although the male juries had utterly failed to successfully handle the liquor question."[16]

After woman suffrage had been in effect in Wyoming for two years, Edward M. Lee, who had been removed as Secretary of the Territory of Wyoming for reportedly being publicly drunk and enjoying the company of "the Circassian Girl,"[17] observed in *The Galaxy* magazine that the power of the ballot had not caused the women to abandon any of their womanly or wifely qualities. As he phrased it:

> With the exception of a few officeholders, the women occupy from a half hour to one day in every year in the performance of public duty at the ballot box, and this trifling deduction of time has not yet disrupted the social fabric, produced chaos or blown society to atoms.

He concluded that the time-honored ordinance of marriage seemed to be as everlasting as the mountains; moreover, there were no signs of that "pestiferous freelove doctrine" which seemed to be gaining converts in the East.[18]

At the 1874 National Woman Suffrage Association convention, the congressman from California, Aaron Sargent, praised the operation of woman suffrage in Wyoming in the following words:

> I might point with some pride to the experiment which has been made in Wyoming, where women hold office, where they vote, where they have the most orderly society of any of the Territories, where the experiment is approved by the executive officers of the United States, by their courts, by the press, and by the people generally; and if it operates so well in Wyoming, where it has rescued that Territory from a state of comparative lawlessness to one of the most orderly in the Union, I ask why it might not operate equally well in the Territory of Pembina or any other Territory.[19]

While Sargent was praising the results of Wyoming women's new found freedom, a number of newspaper editors were questioning the experiment. When the New York *Independent* charged that "scarcely twenty-five women voted in the last election," the *Woman's Journal* investigated and countered with assurances from the Governor of Wyoming and other citizens of the territory that the figure was false. On the contrary, they said the voting of women by 1874 had "become a matter of course." The experiment of granting women a voice in government had been tested for four years when Campbell said he was convinced of the justice and wisdom of the measure. Lecturing in Boston, Edward M. Lee again testified that "no domestic jars" had occurred as a consequence of woman suffrage, even when in one case a husband and wife had been rival candidates for the same office, the one on the Democratic, the other on the Republican ticket. In fact, he said he felt the political situation had improved since the women seemed to vote for the best candidates and were not receptive to bribery.

The fact that women were enfranchised in Wyoming caused Eastern suffragists to be concerned with the events in the Western territory, largely because they wanted to guard women's right to vote where it existed. In January, 1874, when Congress was considering partitioning Wyoming and attaching segments of it to the neighboring territories, New York suffragist Hamilton Willcox spoke against the proposal; his major reason for objecting to the plan was his desire to maintain the existence of the region that was experimenting with woman suffrage. For suffragists, Wyoming was the example to be protected and to be emulated.

In the summer of 1878 when many Eastern newspapers announced "Woman Suffrage is a Failure in Wyoming," the editor of Laramie's *Sentinel*, J. H. Hayford, assured Susan Anthony that most citizens of Wyoming felt the effect of woman suffrage had been "most salutary and beneficial." As he phrased it, *"woman's influence has redeemed our politics."*[20] In 1888, the National Woman Suffrage Association betrayed no doubts in its convention banners which proclaimed: "The vote of women transformed Wyoming from barbarism to civilization."

By this time many suffragists, politicians, and newspaper editors had made inquiries into the workings of the woman suffrage law in Wyoming, and as a result, issued numerous statements declaring the experiment a success. The Cheyenne

Leader assured Easterners that Wyoming was "satisfied with woman suffrage"; while the Laramie *Sentinel* expressed disgust with the mean manner in which men in other states and territories treated their women. The speaker of the Wyoming house of representatives summed up the situation when he declared woman suffrage had "been productive of much good...and no evil."[21]

Generally, Wyoming's territorial governors continued to support woman suffrage. They often accepted invitations to speak to national audiences such as the woman suffrage associations, and on such occasions they praised woman suffrage and promoted the development of Wyoming Territory. In their messages to the Wyoming territorial legislature, the governors frequently praised the operation of woman suffrage. Governor John A. Campbell, two years after his veto of the bill to repeal the woman suffrage statute, boldly assured the Wyoming legislators that the system of impartial suffrage was an unqualified success. In 1875 Governor John W. Thayers told Wyoming's lawmakers that in its six years of practical operations woman suffrage had increased in popularity and in the confidence of the people; thus, he saw no reason why it should be surrendered. Declaring Wyoming the only spot on earth where the political privileges of women were equal and identical with those of men, Governor J. H. Hoyt assured the 1882 legislature that the granting of woman suffrage by the first legislative assembly was a bold and gallant stroke which had turned "eyes of the whole world" on Wyoming ever since. Governor Hoyt's exuberant rhetoric was somewhat exaggerated; yet he accurately observed that woman suffrage in Wyoming had been a happy twelve-year experience which was being effectively used to publicize the territory in an effort to attract settlers and investors. There is no evidence that woman suffrage did attract settlers to Wyoming, but it continued to offer opportunities for promoters to advertise the wonders of Wyoming.[22]

While there was some discussion in the national Congress about disfranchising the women of Wyoming as a spin-off of the antipolygamy campaign in Utah, the example of women voting in Wyoming was lauded at the 1882 American Woman Suffrage Association meeting held in Omaha, Nebraska. Since this conference was staged to initiate the campaign to secure the vote in Nebraska, a special effort was made to spotlight woman suffrage in the American West. Consequently, the governor of Wyoming Territory attended the conference and praised the experience in Wyoming. The Omaha *Herald* reported that Governor Hoyt had assured the suffrage convention-goers that the women of Wyoming Territory took an active interest in any new political cause and exercised their elective franchise purely with a view to the general welfare of the people.

The experiment with woman suffrage in Wyoming was frequently held up as an example wherever efforts were underway to expand the electorate to include women. In 1886, when the suffragists were trying to convince the United States House of Representatives' Committee on Territories to promote legislation for the enfranchisement of women in all the territories and to defeat the legislation designed to disfranchise the women of Utah, Joseph M. Carey, the delegate to Con-

15

gress from Wyoming, was invited by Henry Blackwell to appear before the committee and offer his opinion on the operation of woman suffrage in Wyoming. Admitting he had held no opinion on the subject when the bill had first been passed by the legislature in 1869, Carey told congressmen he was now convinced that "it had been sufficiently demonstrated that women exercised the suffrage as wisely as men." In addition, he "paid a compliment to the women of Wyoming for the interest they took in all public matters, especially the management of the schools and maintained their right to representation."[23] But despite Carey's testimony and suffragists' efforts, nothing came of the campaign to have Congress extend woman suffrage to all the territories. And at the same time, the House Judiciary Committee reported unfavorably on the National Woman Suffrage Association's proposed constitutional amendment designed to enfranchise women in all the territories and states of the nation.

In June of 1889, a delegation of over one hundred Wyoming women met at Cheyenne and demanded of the constitutional convention then underway that woman suffrage be affirmed in the state constitution which was soon to be written. Since the national Congress had taken the vote from women in Utah two years earlier and the courts had nullified the act enfranchising Washington women earlier in 1889, only the women of Wyoming were then citizens in the full sense of the term. During the constitutional debate, the idea of submitting the question of woman suffrage for a separate vote was proposed. Few delegates were willing to openly oppose woman suffrage, but nearly a third of the delegates subscribed to the idea of separate submission, supporting the argument that the people had never had an opportunity to vote on the proposition.

Finally, the woman suffrage clause was included, and two-thirds of the Wyoming voters registered their support of the constitution, which provided that the rights of citizens to vote or hold office should not be denied or abridged on the account of sex.

Even after the vote the debate continued. Answering the detractors of woman suffrage who liked to speculate about the terrible, unfeminine things that would befall women if they were admitted into the political arena, the defenders of the experiment in Wyoming declared that women had not been dragged into politics in spite of themselves. If a woman's inclinations were not in that direction, she could remain at home on election day.

When the Wyoming state constitution was being reviewed in the United States House of Representatives' Committee on Territories, George T. Barnes, the Democratic congressman from Georgia, expressed his opposition to accepting the constitution, and based his objections on the section concerning woman suffrage. In total, twenty-one objections were raised to the woman suffrage clause. Fear that another Republican state would be added to the union if Wyoming was admitted probably motivated the Democrats, and attacking the woman suffrage aspect of the constitution seemed to be a safe approach to blocking the entrance of another Republican state. Problems were also encountered in the Senate. When the proposed constitution was being considered there on June 25, 1890, Senator George G. Vest of Missouri declared he could not vote for it since, in his view, woman suffrage was antagonistic to the spirit of the institutions of the American people. He went on to say that he had deplored the extension of suffrage to black men of the South, but since he considered black women even more "impulsive and thoughtless than the men" he was even more repulsed by a measure which might allow black women to vote.[24]

However, just when it seemed as though the woman suffrage clause would have to be dropped, the Wyoming legislators telegraphed a message to Congress declaring that they would remain out of the union a hundred years rather than join without woman suffrage. Finally, the constitution was approved by a narrow margin with the controversial clause intact.

Immediately, Jane H. Spofford of the woman suffrage association and Women's Christian Temperance Union requested President Benjamin Harrison to sign the bill on July 4, admitting Wyoming as the forty-fourth state. Harrison was on record against woman suffrage in principle; but he signed the bill on July 10, promoting his opponents to accuse him of acting on political expedience since the Republicans felt they needed the political support of Wyoming.

Nonetheless, Wyoming had become the first state to allow its women full voting privileges. In the same year suffragists were further encouraged when the House Judiciary Committee released the first majority report in favor of a proposed sixteenth amendment which would guarantee the right to vote could not be denied on the basis of sex in the same manner that the Fifteenth Amendment protected black men's right to the ballot.[25]

At the statehood celebration in Wyoming, Amelia B. Post, who was designated official representative of the women of the new state, was presented with a copy of the new constitution. Speaking for "the free women of the new commonwealth," Theresa A. Jenkins made the following report to the crowd gathered at the Cheyenne capitol:

> We have never been compelled to petition or protest; we have never been treated with patient hearing, and our practical suggestions have been most courteously received.... Securing in our hands the ballot, may you have no just cause for regret; but may this measure make us more helpful wifes, more womanly women, more patriotic mothers.[26]

One-time justice of the peace Esther Morris was also on hand to present the governor with a forty-four star, silk flag on behalf of the women of Wyoming. Over the years, these women, along with Estelle Kesl, were those in Wyoming who had contact with the national suffragists. More often than not, there was no representative from Wyoming at the national suffrage conventions; but if someone did associate with Eastern suffragists, it was usually one of these four women. The authors of the *History of Woman Suffrage* credited Amelia Post of Cheyenne with being the person "to whom the enfranchisement of the women of Wyoming was

Theresa Jenkins

largely due."[27] However, this tribute may be unearned, since though Amelia Post was frequently present when matters related to woman suffrage were being considered, it was usually men such as Bright, Lee, Kingman, Carey, or Campbell who were writing or signing the necessary legislation.[28]

Once statehood and women's right to vote had been secured in Wyoming, the state legislature and a local newspaper continued to use woman suffrage to advertise Wyoming. Often their commitment to the principle was sincere in that they vowed no harm and much good had resulted from allowing women to vote. Based on this experience, the 1893 legislature urged "every civilized community on earth to enfranchise its women without delay."[29]

However, while demands for the universal enfranchisement of women were being made based on the success of the experiment in Wyoming the antisuffrage associations attacked the example by pointing to reported legal gambling and loose restrictions on liquor traffic in the state where women voted. But the accusations had little backing, and when Alice Stone Blackwell inquired as to their validity, Chief Justice H. V. Groesbeck of Wyoming responded: "The moral tone of our state is improving, owing to the influence of women electors, and we would not discard the 'home element' in our politics if we could."[30]

In May of 1895, suffragist Susan B. Anthony and Anna Howard Shaw briefly stopped in Wyoming to observe for themselves the impact woman suffrage was having. They were the guests at the home of United States Senator Joseph M. Carey, who four years earlier had been the featured speaker at the National American Woman Suffrage Association convention, where he had declared Wyoming the only true republic. When Anthony and Shaw left Wyoming for Utah to attend the Rocky Mountain Suffrage Conference in Salt Lake City, they were accompanied by Theresa A. Jenkins, president of the Wyoming Suffrage Association and suffragist Estelle Kesl.

Wyoming was first, and would continue to be honored by suffragists. As Clara Bewick Colby of Nebraska summarized it in 1897 at the National American Woman Suffrage Association, "No matter if we fill the field of blue with stars [referring to a flag which had a star for each state allowing women the privilege of voting], one will always shine with particular lustre, the star of Wyoming, who opened the door of hope for women."[31] True, Wyoming was in the vanguard, but since the territory's population was small, the experiment was considered by many an invalid example. Moreover, the existence of political rights for women in Wyoming did not result in a vast migration to this "promised land." On the positive side, the woman suffrage law did advertise the existence of the Western territory and women voting proved that there was neither danger nor evil in woman suffrage. One appraisal of the situation in Wyoming was that the women who did take an interest in the questions which were to be settled at the polls seemed to be quite as intelligent in their opinions, judgments, and actions as the men and certainly should be accorded equal rights with the men.

Notes

[1]The most extensive study of woman suffrage in Wyoming has been done by T. A. Larson. The most detailed and thoroughly documented version of his analysis is "Emancipating the West's Dolls, Vassals and Hopeless Drudges: The Origins of Woman Suffrage in the West," in Roger Daniels, ed., *Essays in Western History in Honor of T. A. Larson* (Laramie: University of Wyoming Publications, 1971), pp. 1-16; also see, "Organization of Wyoming Territory and Adoption of Woman Suffrage," in *History of Wyoming,* by T. A. Larson (Lincoln: University of Nebraska Press, 1965), pp. 64-94. A nineteenth century version of the enfranchisement of women in Wyoming was prepared by Hamilton Willcox. This pamphlet was entitled, "Wyoming: The True Cause and Splendid Fruits of Woman Suffrage There from Official Records and Personal Knowledge correcting the errors of Horace Plunkett and Professor Bryce and supplying omissions in the *History of Woman Suffrage* by Mrs. Stanton, Mrs. Gage, and Miss Anthony, and in the *History of Wyoming* by Hubert Howe Bancroft with other information about the state" (New York, November 1890), 28 pages. The events in Wyoming also are detailed in two chapters in *History of Woman Suffrage,* 3:726-48; 4:994-1011.

[2]In the post-Civil War years there was a great deal of concern about surplus women—young women of marriageable age who did not seem to have much of a chance of getting married because there was not an equal number of young men available for marriage. In the more densely populated Eastern United States there seemed to be more young single women than could possibly have a chance for marriage; consequently, efforts were made to encourage them to move to the frontier regions where the sex ratio was usually reversed—more men than women. Yet the census data for 1890 reveals that there were 32,067,880 men in the nation while there were only 30,554,370 women. "For the United States as a whole, therefore, there were for every 100,000 males 95,280 females in 1890. In 1880, there were 96,544 females to every 100,000 males, while in 1870 there were 97,801 females to every 100,000 males." *Deseret News,* 18 August 1892. Thus, it was apparent that the surplus women problem, as it was called, was one of age and geographical distribution, not one of actual numbers. However, even the disproportionate geographical distribution was not as great as might be expected, the 1890 figures show that only in the District of Columbia, Massachusetts, and Rhode Island did the number of women exceed the number of men by more than five percent. Nevertheless, there were numerous newspaper articles dealing with the problem of surplus women.

[3]Governor John W. Hoyt's address on woman suffrage in Wyoming, delivered at Association Hall, Philadelphia, 3 April 1882, on file in the Boston Public Library, is just one of the many testimonies that the bill was not passed to aid women, but to embarrass Governor Campbell. Also see the testimony of the Delegate from Wyoming Joseph M. Carey before the House Committee on Territories on March 20, 1886, as recorded in the *Salt Lake Herald,* 26 March 1886; Judge John W. King-

man's version of the motives in *History of Woman Suffrage*, 3:727-31; and Willcox, p. 14.

[4]Arguments have been presented by historians to show that Bright was persuaded by his wife, by Edward M. Lee, or by Esther Morris to support woman suffrage. All three may have influenced him, but there is evidence that he independently championed the idea. For example, in 1877, when he was living in Denver, he lectured in favor of woman suffrage in the unsuccessful campaign to make women part of the electorate in that new state, and he was one of the seventeen members of a committee appointed to district Colorado and send out speakers.

[5]Ida Husted Harper, *The Life and Work of Susan B. Anthony* (Indianapolis: Bowen-Merrill, 1899-1908), 1:408.

[6]Willcox, p. 13.

[7]From letter of New England Clergyman, D. J. Pierce, as quoted in *History of Woman Suffrage*, 5:739.

[8]*Salt Lake Tribune*, 18 September 1871.

[9]Pauline W. Davis, *A History of the Woman's Right Movement* (New York: Journeymen Printers Co-operative Association, 1871; reprinted ed., New York: Source Book Press, 1970), p. 25.

[10]As quoted in Kathrine Anthony, *Susan B. Anthony: Her Personal History and Her Era* (New York: Doubleday, 1954), p. 248.

[11]Susan B. Anthony 1871 Diary, Anthony Papers, Library of Congress Manuscript Division, Washington, D. C.

[12]*Pacific Coast News*, as quoted in the *Salt Lake Tribune*, 15 July 1871; for details of the Fair controversy, see Harper, *Anthony*, 1:391-95.

[13]Willcox, p. 17.

[14]Willcox, pp. 16-17.

[15]Larson, "Emancipating the West's Dolls, Vassals and Hopeless Drudges," p. 8.

[16]*Chicago Tribune*, as quoted in *Salt Lake Herald*, 6 October 1871.

[17]Larson, *History of Wyoming*, pp. 120-23.

[18]Extract from *The Galaxy* article, 13 (June 1872): [no page] located in Susa Young Gates papers, Widtsoe Collection at the Utah State Historical Society, Salt Lake City, Utah.

[19]*History of Woman Suffrage*, 2:545.

[20]Harper, *Anthony*, 1:496-97.

[21]*Deseret News,* 8 July 1881.

[22]For a discussion of the failure of woman suffrage to attract population, see Larson, "Emancipation of the West's Dolls, Vassals and Hopeless Drudges," p. 8.

[23]As reported in the *Deseret News,* 20 March 1886.

[24]*Deseret News,* 27 June 1890; also see, Willcox, pp. 19-20 and *History of Woman Suffrage,* 4:999-1004.

[25]This amendment which also was referred to as the Anthony Amendment— later the Nineteenth—was modeled after the Fifteenth Amendment and read as follows: The right of citizens of the United States to vote shall not be denied or abridged by the United States or any state on account of sex. Congress shall have the power to enforce this article by appropriate legislation.

[26]Willcox, p. 20.

[27]*History of Woman Suffrage,* 4:295.

[28]For a discussion of who deserves credit for woman suffrage, see Larson, *History of Wyoming,* pp. 89-94.

[29]*Cheyenne Northwestern Livestock Journal,* 17 February 1893; also see, *Rochester, New York, Democrate and Chronicle,* 16 February 1893, in Scrapbook, 1891-1901, Anthony Papers.

[30]Unidentified clipping, 4 May 1897, in Scrapbook, 1891-1901, Anthony Papers.

[31]*History of Woman Suffrage,* 4:282.

II. THE FEMALE FRANCHISE AMONG THE MORMONS

Utah is the land of marvels. She gives us, first polygamy, which seems to be an outrage against 'woman's rights,' and then offers to the nation a 'Female Suffrage Bill'. . . . Was there ever a greater anomaly known in the history of a society?

The Phrenological Journal
November 1871

The territorial assembly of Wyoming made history when it granted the women of that territory the right to vote in 1869. Two months later the women of Utah Territory also were enfranchised. But the experiment with woman suffrage in Utah received much more attention because it admitted nearly forty times as many women to the polling place as had the action in Wyoming; moreover, most of those Utah women were members of a religious faith which practiced plural marriage. In fact some of the women were participants in polygamous arrangements.

Reformers as well as critics intently watched the development of the female franchise among the Mormons. The principal preoccupation of both was: How could what appeared to be the most liberal view of women's rights—suffrage—and the most enslaving marital arrangement—polygamy—develop and coexist in the same environment?

Assuming that woman suffrage and polygamy were inherently antithetical, earlier reformers had suggested that woman suffrage be employed to destroy polygamy. For at least three years prior to the legislation vesting the women of Utah with the political franchise, this idea had been discussed in the East. The United States Congress had gone so far as to consider enfranchising Utah women on the assumption that the women would immediately vote polygamy unlawful. In those days women's right to vote, when discussed by Easterners in relation to Utah, was in fact almost always proposed as a means to eliminate the institution of polygamy.

The assumption, as illustrated by Reconstruction legislation, was that the ballot would be used to free those in slavery from their oppressors. The argument held that plural marriage existed only where women were degraded; therefore, it would disappear if the women were elevated, and political power was the means of elevation. In their zeal to eradicate "the second twin relic of barbarism," many Reconstruction reformers had seized on this idea of having Mormon women vote.

In 1867-68 when New York suffragist Hamilton Willcox had proposed experimenting with woman suffrage in the territories, he gave particular emphasis to the value of testing the idea in Utah. Not only could the system be observed in a territory where there was a large female population, but, as he argued, the Mormon marital system of plural wives also would be eliminated.[1] The New York *Times* popularized this proposal, suggesting that perhaps the enfranchisement of Utah women would result in the casting out of polygamy and Mormonism in general. At the very least, Utah would be a good place to experiment with woman suffrage.

In the spring of 1869, when Congressman Julian's legislation to enfranchise the women of the territories seemed stalled, he again followed Willcox's lead and limited his woman suffrage bill to Utah with the justification that women there would use the ballot to eliminate polygamy. The Utah delegate to Congress, William Henry Hooper, spoke in favor of this proposal, but it never came to a vote.

Generally, this national concern with women in Utah amused the Mormons. Assuring his readers that Utah women could be enfranchised "without running wild or becoming unsexed," George Q. Cannon, editor of the *Deseret News,* the newspaper which served as the official organ of the Mormon church, voiced approval of what he referred to as an opportunity to be an example to the world. The paper also noted that both Mormon men and women already voted in the semiannual general church conferences on all matters brought before the membership.

In 1896, when the subject of the women of Utah was before the national Congress, many Easterners traveled to Salt Lake City on the newly completed transcontinental railroad and returned to the East with tales of the Mormon mecca. As one Christian worker summarized the situation for the *Chicago Advance:* Nearly all the Mormons believed in polygamy but less than one-fourth practiced it; moreover, if the women were left to themselves nine-tenths of them "would vote it so thoroughly out of existence that it would never be heard of again."[2]

The headliners of the period who made political names for themselves, to say nothing of considerable sums of money, by touring the country lecturing on the Mormons, were Anna Dickenson, Kate Field, and none other than President Ulysses S. Grant's Vice President, Schuyler Colfax. Vice President Colfax, who in 1872 was himself the subject of an exposé when the New York *Sun* charged him with accepting stock of the Credit Mobilier in return for political influence, delivered his lecture "Across the Continent" to numerous audiences, including members of Congress. Famous for his public piety the Indiana politician enhanced his nickname, "the Christian Statesman," by his revelations about Mormonism.

Anna Dickenson, herself an advocate of woman suffrage, toured the East after her visit to Salt Lake City in 1869 in the company of the members of the United States House of Representatives' Ways and Means Committee. Her specialty at those appearances was a speech entitled "Whited Sepulchres" in which she depicted the condition of Mormon women as deplorable. As evidence she told of their haggard continence, their dejected looks, and their slavish obedience. A Mormon missionary in Connecticut reported that Anna Dickenson was paid one hundred and fifty dollars for an hour and a-half lecture in which she called for the nation to put down polygamy as it had slavery. In the years after the Civil War, Dickenson had been one of most popular lecturers on the lyceum curcuit, averaging one hundred and fifty lectures a season and earning as much as $20,000 annually. While it was just one of her regular lectures, the "Sepulchres" speech helped make the image of the degraded Utah women one of the most popular images of the day. Reporting the lecture success of the "incorrigible spinster," as Mormon elder John Jacques called her, the *Millennial Star* writer visualized a confrontation between the suffragist lecturer and her "fellow-laborer in the cause of human progress," George Francis Train. He decided they "would make a magnificent team, especially when pulling in opposite directions."[3]

And opposing Anna Dickenson was exactly what George Francis Train did. Train, who had been a friend of Anthony and Stanton during the Kansas suffrage campaign and who had sponsored the suffrage newsletter *Revolution*, countered the critics of the Mormon marriage system in numerous speeches and newspaper articles. After his visit to Salt Lake City in 1869, while campaigning for the United States Presidency, "Citizen" Train, as he like to be called, delivered a speech to two thousand people in New York's Tammany Hall. As an obvious challenge to Anna Dickenson, his oration was entitled "Old Fogies of the Bible and Blackened Sepulchres." That "conglomeration of oddities and eccentricities," as the Mormon press affectionately referred to Train, was a life-long supporter of Mormon virtues and Utah's right to statehood. In fact, he was such an avid defender that he was once asked if he was a Mormon. He answered by declaring he had only one wife and was not a Mormon, but he was not sure that he would not become one. In 1870 while lecturing in the Salt Lake Theatre as Brigham Young's guest, Train jokingly conceded that he never committed adultery and was therefore almost a Mormon, adding, "No wonder they call me a crazy man."[4]

Train's continuing praise of Brigham Young, whom he referred to as the "Napoleon of colonists," won him the unqualified affection of the Mormons. Brigham returned the compliment by describing Train as a gentleman and scholar who had brains and decency even though he would occasionally play the buffoon when it appeared profitable. When Brigham Young died in 1877, Train published a long poem in the Buffalo, New York, *Agitator* commemorating his friend and reaffirming his affection for the Mormons ending with the following play on words:

> And though too *Young* to miss the *Train*
> We *never shall shake hands again!*
> Tell my Utah friends to Hold the Fort
> And I will guarantee support.

Through the years the Mormons were reluctant to be too closely identified with Train because of his wild campaigns in support of Woodhull and Claflin, Fenians, Paris Communards, anarchists, and Young America, and because of his public displays such as protest fasting and his eighty-day whirl around the world which inspired Jules Verne's famous story. Nevertheless, Train continually lauded the Utah experiment with woman suffrage, campaigned for Utah statehood, and generally defended the Mormons against their defamers. But, because of Train's reputation, his defense of the Mormons did not always do them service. As an observer in the Salt Lake City *Tribune* saw it, Train was inclined "to rush in with his mad force...and make Deseret his hobby."[5]

In this period the Mormons attracted supporters who were considered at least

George Francis Train

radical if not the lunatic fringe of Eastern society. Even P. T. Barnum, master promoter of oddities, freaks, and fakes, wrote a letter to the editor of the New York *Tribune* after his trip to Salt Lake valley in the spring of 1870 defending the Mormons against the accusations of Anna Dickenson.

While "the Mormon Question," as the polygamy problem was delicately referred to, was being aired in the press and on the lecture circuit, the idea of experimenting with woman suffrage in Utah became more popular. The stock argument that the vote would cause women to migrate to the territory was not used in the case of Utah, both because the Mormons promoted their marital system as a means to deal with surplus women[6] and because Easterners did not want to encourage more women to move to Utah since it was feared they might become plural wives. On the contrary, the principal ends Easterners hoped would be served by enfranchising the women in the Mormon region were: first, to eliminate polygamy, and second, to experiment with the idea of women suffrage. Even the National Woman Suffrage Association at its 1870 convention resolved that the enfranchisement of the women of Utah was the one safe, sure and swift means to abolish polygamy in that territory.

Responding to the proposed experiment with the female franchise, the Mormon press cynically noted, "It is only the 'Mormons' who will suffer; they will have all the trouble, and the people of the East can look calmly on until the question is settled."[7]

From its inception the proposal to enfranchise the women of Utah was tied to some peoples' desire to eliminate polygamy; consequently, the fortunes of the female franchise in Utah would rise and fall for the next twenty-eight years with the battle over plural marriage. Moreover, women's right to vote would be argued on the local and national scene each time the question of statehood for Utah was considered.

This concern of people outside the territory for women's right to vote in Utah was the most influential force in bringing about the enfranchisement of Utah women. Nonetheless there were woman suffrage advocates in the territory. The first talk of woman suffrage within Utah was heard from a group of liberal Mormon intellectuals who published their ideas in the *Utah Magazine* which developed into the *Mormon Tribune,* and in turn became the core around which the Salt Lake *Tribune* was formed. These Mormon liberals—the principals being William S. Godbe, Edward W. Tullidge, E. L. T. Harrison, Amasa M. Lyman, Henry W. Lawrence, William H. Shearman, and Eli B. Kelsey—created a scheme to end the economic and social insularity of the Mormon community in the Great Basin. At the time of the completion of the transcontinental railroad, these liberals suggested that the Mormons should cooperate with Gentiles[8] to develop manufacturing and mining in Utah. Mormon church officials, however, defended their policy of remaining an agricultural, self-sufficient kingdom. Consequently, there was a conflict with the liberals.[9] The end result was that Godbe and his fellow "new movement" Mormons, as they were called, were excommunicated or voluntarily left the church.

One of the issues championed by the Godbeites was the equality of women.[10] In the subsequent twenty-five years, the Mormon *Deseret News* often credited these liberals with initiating the push for the enfranchisement of women. Politically the Godbeites assumed the roles of a third party in that they introduced liberal ideas— woman suffrage included—which were eventually taken over by the Mormon party.

Why were these liberal Mormon men advocates of woman suffrage? Since all of the principal leaders, except Godbe and Lawrence—who were first and foremost merchants—had served as missionaries in England during the liberal era and since most were directly involved in the editing of the *Millennial Star*, the Mormon newspaper there, it is likely that they had heard the liberal arguments in favor of equality from reformers of the day, such as John Stuart Mill. Godbe, on the other hand, frequently traveled to the East coast to purchase goods for his mercantile enterprises and thus had contact there with the frequently discussed ideas of the day.

Early women's rights activities in Utah centered around the Godbe family. William S. Godbe and three of his four polygamous wives—Annie Thompson Godbe, Mary Hampton Godbe, and Charlotte Ives Cobb Godbe—were active in the women's rights movement. They made the initial contacts with the Eastern suffrage leaders and convened the first meetings in the territory dealing with woman suffrage. Of all the people identified with the Godbeite movement, Charlotte Godbe was the most important figure when it came to woman suffrage.

After William Godbe's excommunication all his wives left the Mormon church except Charlotte, who did not abandon the religion because of her mother. Charlotte's mother was Augusta Adams Cobb Young, Brigham Young's fifth wife, and Charlotte had been raised as one of Young's daughters, even living for a time in Brigham Young's Lion House. Thirty years earlier Charlotte's mother, a member of the prominent Adams family, had fled Boston to become one of Brigham Young's wives and, in so doing, had abandoned her husband and five of her children, taking with her only six-year-old Charlotte and an infant who later died.[11]

Many years later Charlotte wrote to Wilford Woodruff, who was then President of the Church of Jesus Christ of Latter-day Saints, explaining that when her mother had lived in Boston she had been an acquaintance of suffragist Lucy Stone and had maintained contact with her over the years. Charlotte attributed the commencement of woman suffrage activities in Utah to her mother and reported that it had been her mother's death bed wish that Charlotte continue the work she had begun.[12] Charlotte did make woman suffrage her life's work.

In April of 1869, seven months before he excommunicated William Godbe, Brigham Young had sealed Charlotte to Godbe as his fourth wife. This marriage, which Charlotte later referred to as her "painful domestic experience in polygamy," ended ten years later with a divorce after a number of years of separation. Though she did not leave the church, Charlotte was never listed among the Mormon women speaking out for woman suffrage or protesting antipolygamy legislation. The Mormons' refusal to accept her as one of their own may have been as much a result of her spiritualistic activities as the fact that she was married to Godbe. Nevertheless, for many years Charlotte continued her women's rights work independently, largely through letters to editors and feminist speeches. In these early years she also had considerable contact with Eastern suffragists. Nearly twenty years later Charlotte recounted how she had "assumed a prominence among" the women of the national suffrage movement and been elected by them "to speak before the House Committee on this subject, claim for all women the right [to vote]."[13] In 1871 in Boston's Tremont Temple she did speak befcore a large audience on woman suffrage and on the "fine and noble women" of Utah. In doing so, she became the first American woman with voting rights to address Eastern suffragists.

While the ten minutes of her discourse, which she devoted to a defense of Mormon women, earned her the praise of Boston newspapers, they called down the damnation of Emmeline B. Wells, prominent leader of the polygamous women of Salt Lake City and editor of the *Woman's Exponent,* a Utah journal established in 1872 as the explicit vehicle whereby Mormon women could explain themselves to the world and report the labors of their Relief Society. In an article in the *Exponent,* Emmeline discussed Charlotte's unsuccessful polygamous marriage to Godbe and concluded that Charlotte "was not now an advocate for this principle of the Church, hence could not be a representative for the women here [in Utah]." As Charlotte later reported, "the *motive* for this I saw a year after when E. B. W. *tried* to be—what I was—a representative woman in *political* circles."[14]

This contest between Charlotte and Emmeline would persist throughout their long careers. Charlotte was a feminist while Emmeline stood as the symbol of the polygamous wife. Both remained members of the church, and both worked for woman suffrage from their own points of view. Charlotte persisted because, as she often said, it was morally right for women to participate in their government. Emmeline worked for woman suffrage as a means to promote Mormon women, their Relief Society, and such church goals as statehood for Utah. The conflict between these two proud, effective women was constantly being renewed, usually when Charlotte made a feminist statement or observation about Mormon women in the national or suffrage press, which Emmeline generally countered in the *Exponent.*

Like Charlotte, Annie Thompson Godbe also spent her life as an active suffragist in touch with national movement leaders. In fact, she was probably the "Mrs. Godby [sic.], wife of the leading reform advocate of Utah," who with Margaret Lucas, sister of English woman suffrage advocate Jacob Bright was among the distinguished guests at the twentieth anniversary celebration of the inauguration of the women's rights movement held in New York City in 1870. The organizer of the meeting, Paulina W. Davis, concluded, "In Utah it [woman suffrage] is of less account [than the Wyoming example] because the women are more under a hierarchy than elsewhere, and as yet vote only as directed."[15]

Within the ranks of the Mormon faithful there were also those who favored woman suffrage at this early date. In 1868 the editor of the *Deseret News* noted

Jane S. Richards

some justice in women's claim to the right to vote; referring to the recent enfranchisement of black men, he noted women's intelligence and said he saw no reason why they should not also be admitted to the polls. In addition, he speculated, "before long, probably in Massachusettes at any rate, they will have the privilege granted to them."[16] Over the years the *Deseret News* was supportive of woman suffrage. Editors George Q. Cannon and Charles W. Penrose not only used the paper to promote woman suffrage, but often pursued the cause on the lecture platform. Likewise, Franklin D. Richards, who edited the *Ogden Junction* in Utah's second city, supported woman suffrage in both arenas.

Franklin D. Richards and his wife, Jane S. Richards, and his son, Franklin S. Richards, and his wife, Emily S. Tanner Richards would continue to be among the most forceful voices in favor of women's rights heard from within the church. The Richards family frequently hosted Eastern suffragists during their stopovers in Utah, and since Franklin S. was often in the national capital in his role as attorney for the church, he and Emily had occasion to make the acquaintance of prominent suffragists. As a worker for women's rights, Emily would serve on the Board of Lady Managers of the 1892 World's Fair in Chicago and as a delegate to the International Council of Women. Ultimately she would be the initiator of the organization of a suffrage association in Utah.

At the time the question of extending the vote to women was taken under consideration by the Utah territorial legislature in 1870 considerable national attention was focused on the Mormons. Vice President Colfax was carrying out a vigorous anti-Mormon newspaper and lecture campaign. At the same time Congress was inundated with legislation relating to the Mormons. Every mail arriving in Salt Lake City from the East brought news of legislation which appeared threatening to the Mormons. As George A. Smith noted in a letter to his cousin Hannah P. Butler, "I understand about a dozen bills have been presented to the Congress in relation to Utah." These bills varied from schemes to partition Utah, giving segments to the surrounding territories and states, to proposals disfranchising the Mormons, disqualifying them from holding public office and sitting on juries, depriving them of the rights to homestead or preempt public lands, or disinheriting their children.[17] But the legislation that sparked the greatest response in Mormondom was a bill designed to enforce the antipolygamy law of 1862 which was introduced by the chairman of the House of Representatives' Committee on Territories, Shelby M. Cullom.

As Brigham Young assessed the Cullom Bill in a letter to William H. Hooper, Utah's delegate to Congress, "Our sisters here are in high dudgeon over it."[18] The first week of January, 1870, the women of the fifteenth ward in Salt Lake City met to express their opposition to Cullom's legislation. With Sarah M. Kimball presiding, the women unanimously protested the bill and resolved to bring their moral influence to bear against it. A "Sister Smith" even demanded of the governor that women be allowed to vote. At the close of the meeting Eliza R. Snow, who had successively been married to Joseph Smith and then Brigham Young and was recognized as the voice of the Mormon leadership on subjects related to women, suggested that the example of the women of the fifteenth ward be followed by the sisterhood throughout the territory.[19]

On the thirteenth of January, a "great indignation meeting" was held at the old Tabernacle on Temple Square. Despite the inclement weather over 5,000 women of all ages rallied to hear their sisters decry Cullom's "mean, foul" legislation. For the next six weeks women throughout the territory responded to the call to voice their objection to Congressman Cullom's proposal. From Providence in the north to Manti in the south, mass meetings of women were convened to sustain resolutions protesting the proposed legislation. These gatherings demonstrated how effectively the church's organizational structure could be utilized to gather and to display support for a cause. In subsequent years this tactic would be frequently used; moreover, the women soon learned that the sisters of the territory could be quickly and effectively mobilized through the church's ward organization.

Referring to the "great indignation meeting" as one of the grandest female assemblages in all history, the New York *Herald* editorialized:

> It will not be denied that the Mormon women have both brains and tongues. Some of the speeches give evidence that in general knowledge, in logic, and in rhetoric the so-called degraded ladies of Mormondom are quite equal to women's rights women of the East.[20]

Most Eastern newspapers of the day had some positive comments to make about the women of Mormondom as a result of their mass meetings. The New York *Journal of Commerce* confessed that the arguments presented by the women in Utah were fully up the mark of the best efforts of Mrs. Mott, Mrs. Stanton, Miss Anthony, or any other of the female suffrage women who were trying to stir up public sentiment on the eastern side of the Rocky Mountains.[21]

Against this background the Utah legislative assembly considered the advisability of extending the ballot to women. Though the council aired some reservations, after two weeks of discussion the members of the council and house by unanimous vote passed a bill enfranchising the women of Utah.[22] The motives behind the approval of this bill were explained by William H. Hooper, Utah delegate to Congress:

> To convince the country how utterly without foundation the popular assertions were concerning the women of the Territory, some members of the Legislative Assembly were in favor of passing the law; . . .others favored it, convinced of its propriety by the arguments of the friends of that great political reform.[23]

On February 12, 1870, Territorial Secretary S. A. Mann, serving as acting governor, signed into law this act conferring the elective franchise upon women twenty-one years of age or older who had resided in the territory six months, were born or naturalized in the United States, or were the wives, widows, or daughters of native born or naturalized citizens. Though he expressed to Speaker of the House

Orson Pratt his personal doubts as to the wisdom of this legislation, Mann justified his signing of the bill by the unanimous legislative vote.

Acting Governor Mann was not a Mormon, yet he was popular with them.[24] His prompt signing of this piece of legislation endeared him to the women, who quickly convened a meeting and drew up a resolution expressing their appreciation. The resolution was delivered to him by a delegation of women headed by poet Eliza R. Snow. In response, Mann penned a letter philosophizing about the intelligent use of the ballot, and he cautioned that the application of woman suffrage in Utah would "be watched with profound interest, for upon its consistent and harmonious working depends in a great measure its universal adoption in the Republic."[25]

A Mormon faithful, William Clayton was less philosophical when he noted, "the poor, enslaved downtrodden!!! women of Utah can now act for themselves and take revenge on the men of Israel." But as Clayton gleefully observed, those who expected the Mormon women to use the vote against polygamy would "gnash their teeth with rage" and "foam worse than ever," for "there are not many women here but will sustain all the measures of the authorities better than some of the men do."[26]

Once the news was out, messages came in commending the Mormons for their act. "Congratulations. Woman Suffrage, Greenbacks, Protection, Morality, Temperance, Statesmanship, Presidential Platform." So read the telegram sent by that perennial friend of the Mormons, George Francis Train, upon the passage of the bill enabling women to vote in Utah Territory. Brigham Young's reply to 156 Madison Square, New York City, was a cautious, "Family and friends all well. Return congratulations. Truth, liberty, happiness, and mountain air are lovely and desirable."[27] Even the British press commented on female suffrage in Utah. The London *Daily Telegraph* rhetorically addressed its comments to John Stuart Mill and asked how the women of Utah could vote and yet sustain plural marriage, as the "great indignation meeting" appeared to do.

Two days after the act was signed into law, municipal elections were held in Salt Lake City, and according to Brigham Young, twenty-five women exercised their newly gained right to vote. Reportedly, Seraph Young, Brigham's niece, was the first woman to cast her ballot.[28] The New York *Globe* summarized the historical occasion in the following manner:

> A morning dispatch informs us that the women of Utah vote to-day, since female suffrage has become a law in that territory. We expect they will go to the polls in a quiet, orderly, lady-like manner, and deposit their votes without any jeers or opposition from the gentlemen. If this thing can be done in the 'wicked and immoral' city of Salt Lake, where women are supposed to be held in less estimation than they are in the high-toned and healthy cities of New York and Boston, why may it not be accomplished in every town and hamlet in the Union? That the women of Utah will to-day vote to abolish polygamy, we do not expect.

They are as much in favor of that system as the men. It is wrong to expect this of women of Utah, and it will be unfair to call female suffrage a failure if they do refuse to abolish polygamy. The question, however, is not up for decision.[29]

Woman suffrage was a reality in Utah Territory. The Mormon women of the province had registered their dismay with the Cullom Bill and in so doing had, to a degree, sustained the patriarchal family system of multiple wives as practiced by the Latter-day Saints. Now the Mormons were able to say to the world that the women were not held in bondage but were free, consciously and willingly participating in plural marriage. Nonetheless, Senator Cullom continued to push for legislation to abolish polygamy. When the House approved his bill, many newspapers talked of imminent war if the bill became law. Back in "Zion," Mormon military regiments drilled while committees throughout the territory held mass meetings of men and women to draw up remonstrances protesting the pending legislation as tyrannical.[30]

These meetings were well planned and aimed for long-range results. Acting under President Young's direction, Daniel H. Wells corresponded with Delegate Hooper advising him that John T. Caine would be arriving in Washington, D. C., to deliver proceedings of the mass meetings and to assist Hooper with some "efficient aid, by forming public opinion through the press and otherwise, not only paving the way towards the defeat of the Cullom Bill in the Senate, but also in the matter of our admission as a State into the Union."[31]

As agitation against the "second twin relic of barbarism" reached a high pitch in the national capital, even the Godbeites, who had been excommunicated from the church or who had left voluntarily, met with non-Mormon friends at the Masonic Hall in Salt Lake City to draft a memorial to the Senate asking for a modification of the most obnoxious portions of the Cullom Bill as it had been passed by the House. Most attending the meeting voiced their objection to polygamy but noted that the proposed legislation against it appeared to them unjust and overly severe. The United States House of Representatives, however, had approved the bill after amending it to remove the sections empowering the President to send troops to Utah. Moreover, even though Utah women had been enfranchised less than three months, there was a clause added to Cullom's bill withdrawing that privilege. This section of the legislation would have deprived the women of suffrage and the right to serve on juries. Senator Cullom was pushing hard; he had tried to make it the official mission of the Republican party to eradicate polygamy along with slavery. Nevertheless, the Senate adjourned for the summer without acting on the matter.

During that summer, national concern about the Mormons was amplified by the agitation of Reverend J. P. Newman, Methodist preacher and chaplin of the United States Senate, who in reaction to Delegate Hooper's defense of polygamy and the Cullom Bill debates had delivered numerous speeches against polygamy in Washington, D. C. At the height of the summer of 1870, he appeared in Salt

Lake City to challenge Brigham Young to debate the question of whether or not the Bible sanctions polygamy. Brigham Young refused Newman's challenge, but Orson Pratt did present the Mormon view in a debate staged in the Mormon Tabernacle. Upon their return to the national capital, Reverend Newman's wife organized a Woman's Christian Association for the benefit of Utah women with a Mrs. Hollister, Vice President Colfax's sister, in charge of the activities of the association in Salt Lake City.[32]

Six months after the passage of the act permitting Utah women to vote, in the midst of talk of having the female franchise legislation pronounced unconstitutional by the territorial supreme court, the women of Utah went to the polls to cast their ballots in the territorial elections. Despite a considerable amount of what the men referred to as a "good humored chaffing," a large number of women entered the polling places through the separate women's entrances provided for them and cast their votes. A few individualists took their feminism seriously and voted for women for public office. "One lady voted for a lady to be a Commissioner to locate University Lands, also for one to be a Representative in the Territorial Legislature, and for one to be County Treasurer."[33] An observer who was visiting Utah on the occasion of the women's first large-scale experience at the polls, was not impressed. As he saw it, "the Mormon women cared but little for the privilege of voting and cast their ballots just as their Bishops directed."[34]

Doubtlessly many Mormon women were ambivalent about their newly gained political role; some were even openly opposed to women taking part in political affairs. The minutes of women's meetings in the Salt Lake City fifteenth ward of the church reflect the full spectrum of views on voting. Some women clearly declared themselves for women's rights; some said they had little interest in politics but would vote "for good men in office not enemies." Others admitted they had always considered politics beneath the sphere of women, and were thus not interested in voting.[35]

Brigham Young's analysis of Utah women's first experience at the polls was that the ladies of Mormondom had gone "forth in force and voted for the only man who raised his voice in the Halls of Congress in defense of a pluralities of wives"[36] — William H. Hooper. In short, the women had used their political power to affirm the institution of polygamy by reelecting Hooper. It is doubtful that this was a conscious affirmation on the part of women. Hooper was, however, an aggressive advocate of woman suffrage during his days as Utah delegate to Congress.

Reportedly it was Hooper, possibly inspired by Charlotte Godbe, who had proposed the idea of granting women of Utah the franchise in 1869 when the national Congress was considering imposing female suffrage in Utah. Hooper was also credited with engineering the signing of the bill by Acting Governor Mann. The story had it that Hooper, who was in Washington, D. C., at the time the territorial legislature had passed the enfranchising bill, had persuaded Thomas Fitch, the congressman from Nevada, to telegraph Mann to sign the bill. When the duly empowered governor, Wilson Schaffer, who was also in Washington, was about to instruct Mann to veto the bill, Hooper and Fitch convinced him that the whole woman suffrage thing was a hoax. Therefore, no telegram was necessary.[37]

While the Mormons pointed to the reality of women voting in Utah as a refutation of Anna Dickenson's "Whited Sepulchres" and "Woman's Cry from Utah" speeches, Hamilton Willcox, in a *Revolution* article, insisted that women's enfranchisement had sealed polygamy's doom. As he said, Utah women's future was in their own hands; therefore, Congress should let Utah alone. At the same time, the *Revolution* articles objected to the Cullom Bill since it had been altered to take the right of suffrage from the women of Utah.

At this juncture the Mormons repeatedly reminded congressmen that it was in Congress that the idea of enfranchising the women in Utah had been first pursued and that the territorial legislature had passed an enabling act allowing women to vote at the very time that similar measures were being considered in Washington, D. C. "Bah!" was the Salt Lake *Herald*'s response to the frequently heard accusation that the Mormon-dominated legislature had given the women the vote as a means of strengthening their potential power against the non-Mormons.

Most analysts seek the reason for the enfranchisement of Utah women solely in the dynamics within the territory, and most accept the theory that it resulted from an effort on the part of the Mormons to increase their political power to keep control out of the hands of non-Mormons. As Alan P. Grimes argues in his *Puritan Ethic and Woman Suffrage*, "Women voters were not so much pawns in this struggle as reserve troops to be called upon when needed."[38]

One contemporary version of how it happened that Brigham Young, supposedly afraid of the influx of miners into the territory, devised the scheme of granting the right to vote to women, went as follows:

> Capitalists and prospectors multiplied. The wily deceiver then evolved from his narrow soul the magnanimous scheme of *enfranchising the women*. The Mormon legislature passed the bill. The Gentile miners were mostly unmarried men, or had left their families in the East. Every Mormon citizen thus had his civil power extended in correspondence with the numerous alliances.[39]

Certianly, some Mormons may have feared that the territory would be overrun by outsiders once the railroad provided easy access. Nevertheless, at the time the woman suffrage legislation was passed in 1870, the territory's population was 87,000—less than 4,500 of which were non-Mormons.[40] While the *Deseret News* editor admitted that such an influx was possible, as he phrased it, "We do not anticipate such a result." Even when the non-Mormon population had increased, the Mormons securely maintained their political superiority. During the final twenty-five territorial years, the Mormon men alone outnumbered the non-Mormon men four to one. Therefore the theory that women were given the vote so that the Mormons could outvote the non-Mormons is highly questionable. If there were more than four Mormon voters for every non-Mormon voter, it obviously was not necessary to double the Mormon electorate.

Thus these "reserve troops" would never be needed, not even if the men who practiced polygamy (probably around one-fourth the total of Mormon men) were disfranchised. Speculation about the underlying motives based solely on the events within the territory might instead lead to the conclusion that the church leaders, shaken by the liberal schism, were not afraid of growing non-Mormon political power but were questioning their own ability to maintain Mormon political solidarity.

Though motives for enfranchising the women of Utah can be found within the territory and with the Mormon structure, the most compelling reasons were external: the need to counter the downtrodden image of Mormon women and thus stem the tide of antipolygamy legislation, and the desire to find lobbying power and congressional support in the move to achieve statehood. If motives derived from the Mormons' relationship with the larger American society and the federal government are accepted, then Mormon women and Eastern suffragists were pawns, not reserve voting troops as Grimes says. The woman suffrage movement gave the Mormons a national stage upon which they could demonstrate that polygamous wives were intellectual beings capable of thinking for themselves, and thereby willing participants in plural marriage, not the downtrodden slaves painted by lecture-bureau circuit riders. Another important consequence of enfranchising women in Utah was that an army of dedicated lobbyists in the form of Eastern suffragists and prosuffrage congressmen was thereby immediately recruited to the Mormon effort to thwart antipolygamy legislation and indirectly to gain Utah's admittance into the Union.

Notes

[1]In an 1871 article in the *Revolution,* Willcox gave the Universal Franchise Association, of which he was a leading member, credit for woman suffrage in Utah. Three years later in an address before the House Committee on Territories he publicly took credit for originating the idea of enfranchising the women of Utah, and Utah Delegate George Q. Cannon admitted this statement was substantially correct. *Sacramento Union,* 14 January 1874; *Woman's Journal,* 24 January 1874.

[2]*Journal History of the Church,* 5 July 1869, Church Archives, Historical Department of the Church of Jesus Christ of Latter-day Saints, Salt Lake City, Utah.

[3]*Millennial Star* 31 (October 1869): 683. The *Millennial Star* was a Latter-day Saint journal published in Liverpool, England.

[4]*Deseret News,* 23 July 1870.

[5]*Salt Lake Tribune,* 23 November 1871.

[6]In England, as well as in the United States, in the second half of the nineteenth century, there was considerable discussion of what was referred to as the "surplus women" problem. At a time when society was resisting the pressure by some segments to allow women greater independence and greater participation in society, it was concerned about excessive numbers of females compared to the male population. It was as real a problem to Victorian England as the "over-population" of the Isle had been in the Tudor-Stuart period. In a culture that prescribed that women's role was to serve as mother and wife in a monogamous family situation, the fact that there were more women of marriageable age than men was a real problem. Like their seventeenth century ancestors, the nineteenth century English were offered immigration to the New World as one alternative to this problem.

In their proselyting efforts in England, the Mormons capitalized on the problem of surplus women by actively seeking female converts and advertising the opportunities of prosperity and social mobility to be found in the New World; in this case, the New World was the Intermountain Zion. The *Deseret News* printed countless articles on the subject of surplus women and clipped and reprinted stories on the problem from all over the world.

[7]*Deseret News,* 18 March 1869.

[8]Gentile was an expression used by the Mormons to describe anyone outside their faith. Since the terms Gentile and Mormon were in general use at the end of the nineteenth century, they have been adopted for this study.

[9]Leonard J. Arrington, *Great Basin Kingdom: Economic History of the Latter-day Saints, 1830-1900* (Cambridge: Harvard, 1958), pp. 243-44. The July 1871 *Phrenological Journal* ran a detailed biographical article on the "Leaders of the Mormon Reform Movement — with Portraits."

[10]Movement Manifesto and Platform of the Movement published in the *Utah Magazine,* 27 November 1869; the 1869 volumes of the magazine carried a number of articles in support of women's rights.

[11]Mary Cable, "She Who Shall Be Nameless," *American Heritage* 16 (February 1965):50-55.

[12]Charlotte I. C. Kirby to Wilford Woodruff, 16 February 1869, Woodruff Incoming Letters, Woodruff Papers, Church Archives.

[13]Kirby to Woodruff, 5 February 1889.

[14]Ibid.

[15]Davis, p. 25; also see, pp. 4-5.

[16]*Deseret News*, 2 December 1868.

[17]George A. Smith to Hannah P. Butler, 1 February 1870, *Journal History of the Church*.

[18]Brigham Young to William H. Hooper, 11 January 1870, Brigham Young Letterbooks, Brigham Young Papers, Church Archives.

[19]Riverside Stake Fifteenth Ward Relief Society Minutes, 6 January 1870, Church Archives; *Deseret News*, 11 January 1870.

[20]*New York Herald*, 23 January 1870.

[21]*New York Evening Express*, 26 January 1870.

[22]For details of the House and Council consideration and actions of the Ghost Government of Deseret, see Thomas G. Alexander, "An Experiment in Progressive Legislation: The Granting of Woman Suffrage in 1870," *Utah Historical Quarterly* 38 (Winter 1970):25-26.

[23]W. H. Hooper speech in House of Representatives, 29 January 1873, as reported in *Deseret News*, 14 February 1873.

[24]George A. Smith to J. S. Harris, 27 May 1870, *Journal History of the Church*.

[25]S. A. Mann to Eliza R. Snow, Bathsheba W. Smith, Marinda M. Hyde, Phebe W. Woodruff, Amelia H. Young, and others, Mann Papers, 19 February 1870, Church Archives.

[26]William Clayton to Brother Jesse, and Clayton to Brother East, 13 February 1870, Clayton Letterbooks, Bancroft Library, Microfilm at Church Archives.

[27]*Journal History of the Church*, 14 May 1870.

[28]*Deseret News*, 15 February 1870.

[29]*New York Globe*, 14 February 1870.

[30]*Journal History of the Church*, 26, 29 March 1870.

[31]Daniel H. Wells to William H. Hooper, 2 April 1870, Brigham Young Letterbooks.

[32]*Deseret News*, 17 May 1871; *Journal History of the Church*, 8, 12 August; 20 October 1870.

[33]*Deseret News*, 3 August 1870.

[34]Wilford H. Munro, "Among the Mormons in the Days of Brigham Young," *Proceedings of the American Antiquarian Society*, new series 36 (October 1926):229.

[35]Riverside Stake Fifteenth Ward Relief Society Minutes, 20 July 1871; also see 6 January and 19 February 1870.

[36]*Millennial Star* 32 (1870):550.

[37]"William H. Hooper, the Utah Delegate and Female Advocate," *Phrenological Journal,* (November 1870), pp. 330-31; also see Kirby to Woodruff, 5 February 1889.

[38]Alan P. Grimes, *The Puritan Ethic and Woman Suffrage* (New York: Oxford, 1967), p. 41.

[39]U.S. Congress, Senate, 49th Cong. 1st Sess., 1886, *Misc. Doc.* 122:3.

[40]The 1880 census data shows that there were 120,000 Mormons in Utah and 24,000 other residents.

III. UTAH AND THE NATIONAL SUFFRAGE MOVEMENT

For our part, we ought to wish well to the National Woman's Suffrage Convention, for the women have done good things for us, and if they all obtain the suffrage we are satisfied many of them will vote in our favor, that is, in favor of equal rights for the 'Mormon' people, in common with all other citizens.

Editor, *Deseret News*
May 9, 1877

Despite most Eastern suffragists' dislike for polygamy, they lobbied to forestall legislation designed to abolish polygamy, and they indirectly promoted the Mormons' campaign for Utah statehood. The existence of Mormon plural marriage caused national suffragists to be skeptical of woman suffrage in Utah, yet most of the time their skepticism was overshadowed by their desire to enlarge the number of women allowed to vote and to protect woman suffrage wherever it existed.

When Utah women were first enfranchised, Easterners were curious. They wanted to know how the two antithetical ideas of woman suffrge and polygamy could coexist. They wanted to observe firsthand the women who were going to the polls and voting. Were they downtrodden slaves of a religious oligarchy? Were they freethinking feminists? Or, were they something in between?

The leaders of the National Woman Suffrage Association, Susan B. Anthony and Elizabeth Cady Stanton, were two of the first suffragists to travel to the Rocky Mountain West to see for themselves. During their week in Salt Lake City in July of 1871, they lectured on women's rights, drawing crowds of up to one thousand people at a time, and they became acquainted with Utah women. Anthony's 1871 diary reveals that the two suffragists moved back and forth between the Mormon and non-Mormon communities in the city delivering their message of equality and giving their instructions "for the benefit of those who shall engage in the Woman Suffrage Movement in this city."[1] While Anthony usually addressed herself to the political implications of woman suffrage and economic questions such as equal pay, Stanton sparked a greater response with her critiques of marriage and discussions on motherhood.

The afternoon of the second day of their visit, Stanton met for five hours with a large gathering of women in the old Tabernacle on Temple Square. She gave "a brief history of the marriage institution in all times and countries, of the matriarchate, ...of the patriarchate, ...of the polyandry, polygamy, monogamy, and prostitution." Through all this, she reported, "we had a full and free discussion of every phase of the question, and we all agreed that we were still far from having reached the ideal position for women in marriage, however satisfied man might be with his various experiments."[2] After this free exchange Stanton found that "the doors of the Old Tabernacle were closed to our ministrations,"[3] an event she

Elizabeth Cady Stanton

had anticipated for she had talked openly of family planning. Advising her listeners that "quality rather than quantity" should be sought in their offspring, Stanton frankly told the Mormon women "they should not become mothers oftener than once in five years."[4] Continuing, she let it be known that she did not approve of polygamy, but she "thought it less censurable than the practice of keeping mistresses by married men."[5]

Even though Stanton was subsequently barred from the Mormon podiums, the two suffragists continued their discussion of the vital issues at the non-Mormon Liberal Institute. Anthony participated in the dedication of the newly completed meeting house constructed by the Godbeites and "dedicated to the principles of truth and the cause of Human freedom and the universal fraternity of *Man*."[6] Of course, Anthony could not resist provoking the enthusiastic liberal men a little by asking them if they thought the women by their sides approved of all the intervention by man between the women and their God. That evening Stanton had the honor of presenting the first major address in the hall, and she rose to the occasion with her well-known lecture, "The True Republic."

The "motherly" Elizabeth Cady Stanton and the "maidenly Susan B.," as the *Deseret News* referred to the two suffragists, participated in the "Glorious Fourth" of July celebration. Besides viewing the usual parades and displays, they heard a speech by Alexander Majors, famous for his Great Plains wagon-freighting operations with Russell and Waddell. He praised Utah for allowing women to vote and assured the women in the audience that he was confident that they would not make "a less warrantable use" of the ballot than their gentlemen friends.[7] Later in the day Stanton observed the Mormon celebration in the Tabernacle, and though she complained of the disturbance created by the large number of babies and small children in attendance, she admitted "that the thoroughly democratic gathering in the Tabernacle impressed me more than any other Fourth of July celebration I ever attended."[8] Meanwhile, Anthony had gone over to the new Liberal Institute where those "come outers from Mormondom," as she referred to the Godbeites, were rejoicing in their new found freedom. After witnessing the event, she declared that "since the days of Patrick Henry I do not believe the Declaration has been pronounced with such unders[tanding]" as by the people assembled at the Liberal Institute.

After the Independence Day festivities, Anthony dined with the second polygamist wife of William S. Godbe, Mary Godbe, who in the weeks prior to Anthony's arrival, had been hosting a series of woman suffrage meetings in her home.[9] Though there is not specific mention of contact with Charlotte Ives Godbe, who may have been in the East at the time, it is apparent from Anthony's diary that it was the Godbe family, William S., Mary, and Annie, who served as Anthony's and Stanton's hosts during their stay in Salt Lake City. William S. Godbe met the two women at the train depot and took them to their accommodations at the Townsend House. While being escorted around the city and being served dinner at their homes, Anthony became acquainted with the Godbes. Two weeks later, when

Susan B. Anthony, 1871

Anthony was in San Francisco feeling alone in the world after her unfortunate experience related to the Laura D. Fair speech, she recorded in her diary that Godbe had visited and his presence had made her feel "quite at home." Two months later while in the Northwest, she reported having spent a quiet Sunday reading William Godbe's lecture on polygamy and Victoria Woodhull's speech on capital and labor.

Having received rail passes and a plea to hurry to San Francisco from Leland Stanford, Southern Pacific Railroad builder and ex-governor of California, Anthony and Stanton prepared to leave Salt Lake City. Escorted by Emily Pitts Stevens, editor of the San Francisco suffrage paper the *Pioneer,* the two suffragists left Utah territory after a brief stop in Corinne where they delivered short speeches and mailed letters about their trip to Utah. In one of these letters published in the *Revolution,* Anthony concluded that humanitarian men and women everywhere should join in "a simple, loving, fraternal clasp of hands with these struggling women [of Utah, Mormons and Godbeites], and in earnest work with them—not to modify or ameliorate, but to abolish the whole system of woman's subjection to man, in both polygamy and monogamy."[10] As Anthony so often said in those days, women would not be free regardless of the marriage system until they were self-supporting and no longer economically dependent upon men. In her words, "Independent bread alone can redeem womanhood from her curse of subjection to men."[11]

Hannah Tracy Cutler of the American Woman Suffrage Association also visited the Mormon mecca and delivered a suffrage address in the Tabernacle. Returning east with her firsthand observations, she praised the enfranchisement of women in the Western territories and assured suffrage audiences that Reverend Newman had misrepresented the situation in Utah. Woman suffrage was a reality, and it was attracting supporters who wanted to see it continued. Two years after the women of Utah Territory were enfranchised, Congress passed an enabling act designed "to suppress polygamy and allow the people of Utah to form a constitution and a State government." In this enabling act, sponsored by Representative Aaron A. Sargent of California, woman suffrage was protected by the following provision: "All persons qualified by law to vote for representatives to the general assembly of said Territory of Utah at the date of the passage of this act shall be qualified to be elected." As the bill continued, "they are authorized to vote for and choose representatives, to form a constitution...and also to vote upon the acceptance or rejection of such a constitution."[12] Acting on this invitiation, the citizens of Utah drew up a constitution which was acclaimed by George A. Smith as a most thoroughly republican document. As Smith said, it gave every American, without respect to color or sex, the right of franchise.[13]

While Henry B. Blackwell, in the Boston-based *Woman's Journal,* applauded the constitutional convention as the first one ever elected by the united suffrage of men and women, the New York *Times* lauded the 1872 constitution as being very liberal, perfectly republican, and eminently progressive.

Ironically, it was the group of Mormon liberals, now separated from the church, who had originally been advocates of woman suffrage who now found themselves in the awkward position of opposing the new constitution. They feared Utah would be allowed to join the union with polygamy intact. Four hundred women of Utah, headed by Cornelia Paddock, Jennie Froiseth, and Annie Godbe and Mary Godbe, petitioned Congress through the well-known anti-Mormon crusader, Vice President Schuylar Colfax, to deny Utah's admittance to the Union; because, as they said, statehood would result in the withdrawal of the safeguard of the federal government, which they felt was vital for the protection of their rights. As Cornelia Paddock noted in 1972 in her book on Mormonism, *The Fate of Madame La Tour*, there were not many non-Mormon women in Utah, and most of the signers of the petition were women who had once been active Mormons.[14] Later some of the Mormon women who had signed the petition publicly withdrew their names, saying they had been misled as to the memorial's meaning.

Years later, the Godbeite, Henry Lawrence analyzed the enactment of the woman suffrage measure in the following manner: The liberal movement in Utah was growing and "so sensible was the Priesthood [of the church] of this fact, that the right of suffrage was granted the Mormon ladies by its leaders in order to swell the list of church voters."[15] Yet within a year after the bill became law, the liberals were convinced that woman suffrage was "another polygamic institution." The liberals saw that woman suffrage was being employed as a barricade against the onslaught of antipolygamy attacks. In addition, Mormon women and woman suffragists were being tied together. As another observer exclaimed, "The woman's rights women and the Mormon sisterhood [were] drawn together by strong sympathies and peculiar thoughts and practices." This same commentator noted that the woman suffragists would, unwittingly or otherwise, facilitate Utah's admittance to statehood. In his words:

> There is. . .[a] class who, if possible, will handmaid our State into existence with the polygamic compromise, namely that of the 'woman's rights' wome, nled [*sic*] by such innovative spirits as Victoria Woodhull, Mrs. Tracy Cutler, Elizabeth Cady Stanton and Susan B. Anthony. These have all their peculiar social and political schemes, such as female suffrage, the reconstruction of the relations between the sexes and the general remoulding of society.[16]

While Congress was considering granting statehood to Utah, another piece of legislation denying the vote to the women of Utah was introduced in the United States House of Representatives. Publicized as a bill "to promote the purity of elections in the territory of Utah," it provided that only male citizens over the age of twenty-one should be allowed to vote.

As questions of Utah statehood and woman suffrage continued to be discussed in Congress, the Republican party held its convention and drew up a party platform. The national party leaders rejected Henry B. Blackwell's request for a plank in support of woman suffrage with the plea that the party already had too many causes, and until some of those goals were attained the party was not prepared to take up another.[17] The final Republican platform in 1872, however, contained what some referred to as a splinter in favor of woman suffrage embodied in a vague statement that the party was mindful of its obligation to the loyal women of America for their noble devotion to the cause of freedom and their honest demands for additional rights were declared worthy of respectful consideration. Weak as it was, this was the first comment on the subject in a major national political platform. Moreover, 1872 was the first year a Republican party convention was held in Utah Territory. Though many of the leaders at the Utah Republican party convention were men known to be sympathetic to the idea of the vote for women, the strongest statement put forth in their platform was an affirmation of "the inviolability of the right of suffrage."

Woman suffrage was not making much headway on the national political scene. Nevertheless, Utah women continued to vote. Noting that after their third opportunity to participate in a general election, both Mormon and non-Mormon women in Utah seemed to be voting, out of free choice, for the ticket supported by their husbands, the *Chicago Post* editorialized that woman suffrage did not appear to be any more of a cure-all for Mormonism or a panacea for polygamy than for any of the other sundry ills to which the political doctors of the day would apply it. Some journalists attempted to use "the example of Utah in the matter of women voting to prejudice the minds of the people against woman suffrage." But the Salt Lake *Tribune* editor cautioned that this argument was unsound "for the reason that Mormon women in Utah vote[d] by the dictation of the Priesthood the same as the men." As he saw it the example of woman suffrage in Utah should not be used to discredit the national movement because the right of suffrage in Utah was not exercised in "that free and untrammelled manner contemplated by the advocates of the woman suffrage movement."[18]

Some suffragists, nonetheless, were more defensive about the experience with woman suffrage in Utah. Emily Pitt Stevens, editor of the San Francisco *Pioneer*, concluded that Mormon women, blinded by ignorance and prejudice, were powerless. Writing under the pseudonym "H. H.," Helen Hunt Jackson, author of the early Indian right's treatise, *A Century of Dishonor*, and the popular novel, *Ramona*, explained that the apparent subservience of the good Mormon women rested on their belief that salvation of their souls was only possible through polygamy.

Elizabeth D. Kane, wife of the long-time friend of the Mormons, Pennsylvanian Thomas L. Kane, had occasion on her 1872 tour through Utah Territory to get a feeling for the women's attitudes toward politics. In a letter posted in Fillmore, Elizabeth Kane wrote to a friend, noting that without a doubt the women of Utah voted. "True; but," as she said, "they do not take more interest in general politics than you do." Then she went on to explain:

> If your husband, Charlotte, your father, brothers, and all the clergymen you know, approved of your voting, it would not strike you as an

unfeminine proceeding. And if the matter on which your vote was required was one which might decide the question whether you were your husband's wife, and your children legitimate, you would be apt to entertain a determined opinion on the subject.

She ended her letter with observation:

Nobody thought us unfeminine for being absorbingly interested in our national affairs during the war. The Utah women take a similar interest in the business of the world outside that concerns *them*; and pray over congressional debates as we prayed for our armies.[19]

Another Eastern traveler to the Rocky Mountains, John S. Hittell, concluded that the women of Utah were satisfied with their situation in life. Compared with women in other parts of the United States, they did not seem to be discontent. His analysis of woman suffrage was that the Mormon men had shown their confidence in their women by conferring on them the right of suffrage mainly as a protection against "the Gentile agitators," who he reported had no wives in the territory.

Whatever the motive, woman suffrage was a fact in Utah in 1872, and the men of Utah seemed willing to go beyond suffrage in the area of women's rights. Two women lawyers were certified to argue in Utah courts. Admitted to the Utah bar on the same day were Phoebe W. Couzins, a national suffrage leader and recent graduate of the law course at Washington University in St. Louis, and C. Georgia Snow, a Utah woman who had read the law in the office of her father who held the post of attorney general of the territory.

Throughout the nation the 1870s were characterized by unrest and extremes in women's rights. Having rejected a woman suffrage bill, the Massachusetts state legislature was petitioned by 162 women of Lowell to legalize polygamy. To the horror of many Easterners and to the amusement of the Mormons, the latter petition made it seem to some that plural marriage was gaining ground as the solution to the surplus woman problem. The earlier joining of the issues of woman suffrage and polygamy seemed for a moment to be turning on the Easterners. The whole matter, however, was quickly dismissed by the Massachusetts lawmakers and was subsequently forgotten.

In Rochester, New York, officials were having a difficult time dealing with Susan B. Anthony when she refused to post bail upon her arrest for having exercised what she said was her right to vote according to the Fourteenth and Fifteenth amendments.[20] City fathers relieved themselves of the awkward prospect of having to jail Anthony until her trial by freeing her on her own recognizance. Indicted for illegally voting, Anthony was ultimately tried in United States district court and fined $100, which she refused to pay. When no effort was made to enforce the ruling, she was robbed of the chance she had hoped for to pursue the case to the Supreme Court.

New York City officials, on the other hand, had no such qualms about arresting

1871 Women's Delegation before House of Representatives' Judiciary Committee. Victoria Woodhull speaking.

Victoria Claflin Woodhull, radical feminist and the 1872 Equal Rights party candidate for the presidency of the United States. Charged with circulating obscene literature through the mails in violation of Anthony Comstock's moral censorship laws, she was taken into custody as she was leaving Cooper Institute where she had been the guest lecturer. While the authorities were hauling her away, she made it clear that her thoughts were not only with her conflict with Anthony Comstock's sense of morality. She said she feared that Congress would not do anything for woman suffrage that session since the judiciary committee, which she had addressed the year before, now seemed unanimously against women voting even in the territories.

As Woodhull knew, the committee had been preoccupied for over five years with the subject of woman suffrage in the territories. Some of the legislation discussed in their chambers favored enfranchising all women in the territories and allowing them to hold office as an experiment, but these bills were usually dismissed by a majority of the congressmen on the grounds that they would be interfering with the internal operations of the territories. These same congressmen, however, did not hold local sovereignty so sacred when it came to intervening in the territories in order to take the vote from women. Most of the measures released from the committee on the subject were attempts to disfranchise the women of Utah.

The most extreme example of this type of legislation was the Frelinghuysen Bill "in aid of the execution of the laws of the Territory of Utah, and for other purposes": the "other purposes" being to exclude women from juries and annul the act enfranchising the women of Utah. This proposal of the Republican Senator from New Jersey, presented in response to President Grant's request for legislation for the enforcement of law in Utah, went so far as to attempt to prohibit future territorial legislation or constitutions from allowing for woman suffrage. This bill would not only deprive the women of Utah of the ballot they already possessed, but was originally designed to disfranchise the women of *all* the territories, to forbid them to serve on juries and to subject them to the provisions of the English common law "as it existed before the Declaration of Independence." As Senator Frederick Theodore Frelinghuysen advised Vice President Henry Wilson, the judiciary committee, after long deliberations, dropped the part about the common law and limited the bill to Utah. As further explanation he attributed the authorship of the original bill to "a delegate from one of the Territories, conversant with the difficulties in Utah."[21]

After a year of intermittent debate on the Frelinghuysen Bill, it was passed by the Senate but defeated in the House as a result of the aggressive opposition of the congressman from California, Aaron A. Sargent, who had been responsible for the 1872 enabling bill, which had gone to great lengths to protect the voting rights of Utah women in the constitution writing process. Sargent was supported in his effort to defeat the Frelinghuysen Bill and other proposals to disfranchise women by other friends of woman suffrage, particularly George A. Hoar and Benjamin F. Butler from Massachusetts, and C. W. Willard of Vermont, who were peti-

Aaron A. Sargent

tioned on the subject by Eastern woman suffrage associations.

Attacks on the political rights of women in Utah seemed to be justifiable, not because they were voting, but because they had not employed the ballot to destroy polygamy. The fact that the subject was never placed before them for a vote seemed of little importance. The rhetoric of the day revealed a belief that there was something so magical about enfranchisement that once granted suffrage, any segment of society could use the vote to remodel the world to conform to its own views. In a speech in the House of Representatives, Utah Delegate Hooper asked a congressman from Montana why he really objected to the Utah woman suffrage bill: "Is it because the women vote, or because they do not vote as the gentlemen would have them?"[22]

Once it became apparent that the women of Utah were not going to vote down polygamy, other ballot-based solutions were proposed. Schemes were put forth to import New Englanders to Utah, to import Methodists, to import blacks, or to disfranchise the Mormons. All these ideas rested on the assumption that polygamy would be eradicated at the ballot box if the political structure of Utah could somehow be altered. One feminist proposed another political solution when she suggested disfranchising all the men of the territory and allowing only women to vote.[23] This proposal did not receive much more attention than the whimsical suggestion that *Harper's Baazar* magazine be sent to Utah, thus instilling in Mormon women a desire for high fashion and consequently making it financially infeasible for a man to maintain more than one wife.

While these proposals only received passing attention such unreasonable legislation as Senator Frelinghuysen thought necessary incensed women's rights advocates throughout the country. Woman suffrage associations from New England to California worked actively to defeat this measure. At the sixth annual convention of the National Woman Suffrage Association, Elizabeth Cady Stanton termed the legislation an insult to the women of the Union and a disgrace to the Forty-Third Congress. A representative of the Pennsylvania Woman Suffrage Association argued that if suffrage could be taken from women, then it should be taken from men for the same reason. Expanding upon this theme, Henry Blackwell pointed out that if any class of Mormons should be disfranchised for practicing polygamy, it certainly ought not to be the women. The *New York Independent* reinforced Blackwell's stance when it noted that if Senator Frelinghuysen's argument was taken to its logical conclusion, then it was "the all-too-much married men" of the territory who should be denied access to the ballot — indeed, all who professed the Mormon religion.

When Frelinghuysen's bill was reintroduced in the subsequent congressional session, J. H. Willcox, the representative of the New York Woman Suffrage Association, again appeared before the House Committee on Territories and spoke for his allotted thirty minutes in favor of woman suffrage. He argued that there had not been a fair trial of woman suffrage in Utah and would not be until there was a secret ballot in the territory. Moreover, the campaign by Lucy Stone and Henry

B. Blackwell in the *Woman's Journal* publicized the manner in which the women in Utah were being treated by many of the nation's leaders. On the occasion of the centennial anniversary of the Boston Tea Party, Mr. Blackwell spoke before the New England Woman Suffrage Association, reciting the positive aspects of woman suffrage in the territories. The meeting ended with a resolution calling on Congress to defeat the Frelinghuysen Bill.[24]

During the 1874 congressional session, the subject of woman suffrage was frequently on the agenda. Petitions protesting the disfranchisement of women of Utah were presented by women's groups from New England, California, Ohio, Pennsylvania, and Indiana. One of the Radical Republican Charles Summer's last congressional actions before his death was to present a petition on behalf of the Woman Suffrage Association of Pennsylvania protesting Frelinghuysen's Bill and similar legislation which reintroduced the idea of imposing the common law on Utah women. On the positive side, the former congressmen, now senator, from California Aaron A. Sargent, presented a petition in the Senate from the Woman Suffrage Association of California asking the adoption of an amendment to the United States Constitution declaring that the right to hold office should not be denied on the basis of sex and that the laws of the District of Columbia and territories should be amended to allow women to vote, hold office, and exercise all rights under the law as were then exercised by men.

Later Benjamin F. Butler attempted to persuade the House Judiciary Committee to strike the word "male" from the qualifications for voters in the District of Columbia. When he presented his proposal, Butler was accompanied by Susan B. Anthony, who chided the committee to at least report a bill relieving the unfranchised women of the District of Columbia from taxation.

Also testifying that day was Sarah J. Spencer, who three years before had been referred to the courts by the judiciary committee for resolution of the question regarding the voting rights of women citizens in the District of Columbia. Now she was returning to report to them that the Supreme Court of the District had decided that women had the right to vote but that right could not be exercised except by the aid of express legislation. Sarah Spencer asked for such legislation, saying she knew personally that a large part of the most enlightened and cultured ladies in the District desired the elective franchise. With the reference to the argument that "the bad women would all vote," she said, "the bad women were mostly too young to vote."[25] Also arguing for women's rights before the committee were two women lawyers: Phoebe Couzins, who had been admitted to the bar in Missouri, Utah, Kansas, and Dakota Territory, and Belva A. Lockwood, who had recently been admitted to the bar of the District of Columbia after she had demanded that President Grant, who was ex-officio president of the National University Law School, issue her diploma for the law course she had completed in May 1873. The result of the debate on the expansion of the District of Columbia electorate was that women were not permitted to vote, and all men lost the franchise when Congress abolished the District's territorial status in 1874.

Subsequently, in almost every congressional session there was some proposal attacking polygamy which included a clause to take the ballot from the women of Utah. In 1876 Belva Lockwood referred to such disfranchising legislation and advised the National Woman Suffrage Association that "our most sacred rights [have] been made the football of legislative caprice."[26] Subsequently, she presented a resolution for association approval denouncing the proposition about to be again presented to Congress for the disfranchisement of what she referred to as thousands of legal voters in that territory, and she suggested that the chairperson of the convention, Matilda Joslyn Gage, appoint a special committee of three persons "to memorialize Congress and otherwise to watch over the rights of the women of Utah in this regard." Upon passage of the resolution the chair complied with Lockwood's suggestions appointing a group to work with Congress on the Utah women question. The committee consisted of Lockwood, Sarah J. Spencer, and Ellen C. Sargent, wife of Aaron A. Sargent, the prosuffrage senator from California.

The American branch of the woman's movement also persisted in admonishing Congress on its attitude towards women voting in Utah. In the pages of the *Woman's Journal*, Henry Blackwell frequently reminded Republican congressmen of their party's 1872 platform statement favoring women's rights. He also warned that if the Republicans now disfranchised the women of Utah, the nation's women would question the party commitment to women and would react in an "appropriate manner" to Republican candidates for public office. Despite all these veiled threats and arguments in favor of woman suffrage, various versions of Frelinghuysen's bill and a half dozen similar pieces of legislation, all centering on women's right to vote in Utah, continued to be discussed in congressional committee rooms and on the floor of the Senate and House.

Infuriated by the irrational arguments they heard to justify taking the vote from Utah women, suffragists asked congressmen how they could pretend to take the vote from Utah women as a means of destroying plural marriage while all the time continuing to allow male polygamists to vote. Going even further, Henry Blackwell, who had been a persistent crusader for abolition and equal rights, admonished them saying: "The utter indifference of Congress to the rights of women in Utah is in singular contrast to its almost morbid sensitiveness in regard to the rights of colored men."[27]

While the national suffrage organizations and the friends of woman suffrage in Congress were fighting to keep the women of Utah from being denied access to the polling booth, the question of women's right to hold public office was being tested in Utah. By running for county superintendent of schools on the Mormon ticket, the People's party, Mary E. Cooke stimulated a lively debate as to the eligibility of women to hold office in the territory. Finally, conceding defeat to those who argued that the territorial Organic Act made reference to officeholders by referring to "he", and that the right to hold office could not be implied from the right to vote, the People's party central committee withdrew Miss Cooke's name and

Ellen Clark Sargent

replaced it with a respectable male substitute. On other occasions women were nominated for such offices as county treasurer, but the party's central committee repeatedly ruled them ineligible for office.

Capitalizing on the popularity of the cause of Utah women with Eastern suffrage organizations, Utah's delegate to Congress George Q. Cannon, aided by Senator Sargent, delivered a memorial to the Forty-Fourth Congress signed by 26,626 Mormon women requesting repeal of the 1862 antipolygamy law. In addition, the women requested statehood for Utah and the right of married women to file homestead and preemption claims in their own names.

Later when yet another bill was introduced in the Senate to regulate the elective franchise in Utah by disfranchising all the women and those men of the territory who had entered into plural marriage since the passage of the 1862 antipolygamy legislation, Mary A. Reynolds of Utah wrote to the *Woman's Journal* appealing to the women of America to help stop the enactment of such unfair and unconstitutional legislation. At about the same time, the representatives of the National Woman Suffrage Association, Lockwood and Spencer, appeared before the Committee on Territories attempting to thwart this latest threat to Utah women's right to the ballot.

In the wake of continued antipolygamy legislation in Congress which was almost always formulated in terms of disfranchising women, the Mormon women of the territory continued to cultivate their ties with the national suffrage movement. Emmeline B. Wells sent Brigham Young copies of articles she had submitted to the *Woman's Journal* of Boston saying she thought they would improve the image of women and polygamy in Utah. However, she assured him that as she acted as a representative of the interests of women of Utah she knew she would "sometimes need to draw wisdom from the *Fountain Head* of God's Kingdom on the earth."[28]

Independent feminist Charlotte Godbe also defended both polygamy and woman suffrage in Utah in her contacts with Eastern suffragists and in letters to the *Woman's Journal*. At times, however, Emmeline B. Wells felt it necessary to qualify and correct Charlotte's often unorthodox feminist statements.[29] Reacting to Emmeline's comments, Charlotte charged, "She has systematically misrepresented me, and never has my name appeared in her little paper [the *Woman's Exponent*] with credit."[30] While Charlotte and Emmeline continued to snipe at one another, the National Woman Suffrage Association was attempting to unite all women around the centennial celebration of the American Revolution.

On the Fourth of July 1876, Susan B. Anthony forced her way into the centennial celebration at Philadelphia's Independence Hall and delivered a Declaration of Rights of Women of the United States to the gathering that had refused her request to be on the program. Later, suffragists at the 1877 National Woman Suffrage Association endorsed this declaration and requested that the nation begin its second century of existence by passing a constitutional amendment declaring women's right to the ballot. This measure, commonly known as the Anthony

Amendment, was presented to Congress by Senator Sargent. The proposal would, forty-three years later, become the Nineteenth Amendment to the Constitution.

The National Woman Suffrage Association sent a circular to Utah requesting support in this amending endeavor. In response, the Mormon women called a meeting at the office of the *Woman's Exponent* where plans were formulated to canvass the territory for signatures favoring this proposed sixteenth amendment. The Mormon press treated the petition for the proposed amendment as a sustaining of woman suffrage and as a means to perpetuate the privilege in Utah Territory rather than as a measure to extend the franchise to all women of the nation. These were the circumstances which provoked the *Deseret News* to editorialize: "For our part, we ought to wish well to the National Woman's Suffrage Convention for the women have done good things for us, and if they all obtain the suffrage we are satisfied many of them will vote in our favor . . . ."[31] Ultimately, over 13,000 signatures in favor of the amendment were gathered in Utah through the Relief Society organization and forwarded to the national capital.

Liberals and ex-Mormons such as Annie and Mary Godbe did not sign this petition. Yet Annie and Mary persisted in their faith in the principle of woman suffrage, and they continued to have contact with the national suffrage organization. Annie was the National Woman Suffrage Association vice president representing Utah at the annual conventions, and Mary served on the executive committee. Yet they shared the antipolygamists' belief that woman suffrage should be withdrawn from Utah until plural marriage was discontinued.

The liberal non-Mormon population of the territory which had placed so much hope on the enfranchisement of Utah women before the enabling legislation was passed, now, eight years later, was sending their emissary, Judge Joseph Hemingray, to Washington, D. C., to lobby for the repeal of women's right to vote in Utah. Once the liberals saw how effectively the Mormons were using woman suffrage to recruit lobbyists against antipolygamy legislation, the liberals declared that woman suffrage should be discontinued in Utah. Judge Hemingray appeared before the House Committee on Territories to testify in favor of the Luttrell antipolygamy bill, which like so many of its predecessors contained a clause disfranchising the women of Utah. However, Hemingray's efforts were countered by the resident congressional committee of the National Woman Suffrage Association. The suffragists who were assigned at that time to lobby Congress on behalf of Utah women's right to the ballot were: Sarah Spencer, the lady who had taken the question of female franchise to the Supreme Court; Isabella Beecher Hooker, sister of famed preacher Henry Ward Beecher; and Dr. Mary Walker, the Civil War doctor to whom Congress had granted the special privilege of wearing trousers and caring for the medical needs of soldiers during the Civil War.

As George A. Cannon reported, these national suffrage women "said many things which fell better from woman's lips than they would have from mine." The woman suffrage cause, as Cannon analyzed it, was the one then "looming up in politics"; consequently, these women were wielding considerable influence. Moreover, he noted that they could be cultivated by the sisters of the church with advantage. He assured John Taylor, who had succeeded Brigham Young as head of the Mormon church upon Young's death, that the correspondence of Emmeline Wells and others with national suffragists had "done good."[32] The strategy of the Mormon hierarchy to recruit the women's rights advocates to their side of the battle in Congress was succeeding. Writing to "Dear Uncle" John Taylor, Delegate Cannon acknowledged that whenever Congress tried to get at polygamy by striking down female suffrage it rather pleased him; for he knew it would call the woman suffragists to the Mormon's aid.[33] As Cannon pointed out, the idea of woman suffrage seemed to be growing in popularity throughout the country, and the Mormons took comfort in the fact that Congress was becoming less willing to abolish it where it was already established even though individual congressmen did not favor women voting.

After reexamining the voting laws of the territory, the 1878 Utah territorial legislature sustained woman suffrage and passed measures providing for a secret ballot and registration of voters. While the secret ballot was accepted by the non-Mormon Liberal Party, it rejected the idea of registration and the franchise for women.

With the vote for women reaffirmed, women took a more active role in politics. Urging consistency, the *Deseret News* editors stated their position: "We believe in the right of woman to occupy every position for which she is adapted by nature and qualified by education and experience and no other."[34] Though the People's [Mormon] party did not push to have a female on the ballot after the Mary E. Cooke incident, a number of women did serve as delegates to the party's convention. Mrs. D. W. Smith and Emmeline B. Wells were even elected to the central committee from Salt Lake county in 1878. Of the seventy-seven delegates to the territorial convention of the People's party that year, seven were women.

The franchise as viewed by the Mormons was not an innate human right as expressed in the liberal credo; rather it was a privilege bestowed upon some citizens by the governing body. This frequently reiterated stance was in direct opposition to the philosophy of the National Woman Suffrage Association, as was the Mormon insistence that suffrage was a local, not a national, issue. The Mormon view was exemplified in a critique of the association's newspaper, *The National Citizen and Ballot Box*. In response to suffrage editor Matilda Joslyn Gage's plea for the adoption of the Anthony Amendment and her claim that suffrage was a right of all women by their citizenship, the *Deseret News* editor advised the association that rather than attempting to convince congressmen to amend the federal constitution, it should be concentrating on persuading the legislative bodies of each state and territory to grant the ballot to its women. In short, franchise was a privilege conferred, not a right inherited, and the conferring power belonged to the states and territories.

Almost the only Mormon argument which took exception to the states' rights stance was the position of some leaders that since the Constitution had been amended to provide that the right to vote should not be abridged on account of race, color, or previous condition of servitude, there seemed no reason why the right to vote should be abridged on account of sex. Moreover, vocal Mormons cautioned idealists that the conferring of the vote upon women could not effect such a wonderful evolution of society as the prominent advocates of women's rights might imagine.

Philosophically, the Mormons were much closer to the Boston-based, states' rights oriented American Woman Suffrage Association. Nonetheless, it was the National Woman Suffrage Association to whom they looked for championing their cause in the national capital. Simply because of their philosophy of working at the national level, it was the New York-based suffragists who were continually lobbying in Congress. Seldom did the American Association suffragists try to persuade Congress, but their *Woman's Journal* frequently publicized the problem of woman suffrage in Utah and served as a forum for Mormon women to present their case.

Non-Mormon Utahns tried repeatedly to take their case directly to Congress or the President. Governor Emery of Utah Territory and Salt Lake City's antipolygamy women asked Congress to abolish woman suffrage in the Mormon domain. In addition to petitioning Congress, the women of Salt Lake City's Congregational Church also sent out pleas to the women and clergy of the country and to Mrs. Rutherford B. Hayes to assist them in their battle against polygamy.

George Q. Cannon, acting under instructions from church president John Taylor, tried unsuccessfully to obtain the names of the 2,000 Utah women who had placed their signatures on the antipolygamy petitions addressed to Mrs. Rutherford B. Hayes and to Congress. As part of their counter to the antipolygamy women, the Mormon women of Utah Territory once again activated their petitioning machinery and convened numerous meetings throughout the territory.

Once the signatures were secured on the petitions, two Mormon women took them to the nation's capital. The same year Mormon women were sent to the National Woman Suffrage Association convention for the first time. Prior to 1879 the Godbe women had been the only Utah women at these conventions. Mary Godbe was still listed as a member of the association's executive committee, but Emmeline B. Wells was now designated honorary vice president representing Utah. When Emmeline and Zina Young Williams, daughter of Zina D. H. Young and Brigham Young, departed Salt Lake City to journey to Washington, D. C., for the convention, they were acclaimed as "representatives of plural marriage as well as other woman's rights."[35] In addition to attending the suffrage convention, they were commissioned to deliver the Mormon women's petition to President and Mrs. Hayes, and to again memorialize Congress to repeal the 1862 antipolygamy legislation which had been declared constitutional by the decision of the Supreme Court in the George Reynolds case. As part of the national woman suffrage delegation, Emmeline and Zina called upon President and Mrs. Hayes and requested the legitimization of the children of plural marriage and urged that the 1862 act against polygamy not be enforced.[36]

On the other hand, Matilda Joslyn Gage and Sarah J. Spencer of the National

Woman Suffrage Association tried to make it clear to the First Family that the association should not be construed as taking part in any other branch of the Mormon question except that of woman suffrage. They contended that although the women of Utah already had enjoyed the right to vote for nine years, Congress, which had repeatedly refused to interfere with state or territorial governments to grant suffrage to women, was now contemplating interfering to take it away from the women of Utah.[37]

The Mormon women's plea to the President and Mrs. Hayes apparently had little impact because in the 1879 annual address to Congress, President Hayes announced that he agreed that the most effective means of dealing with polygamy was to disfranchise the plural married people and prohibit them from sitting on juries. Contending that this was a cowardly way to fight polygamy, the Salt Lake *Herald* noted that disfranchisement should not be inflicted upon anybody who has not been convicted of a crime.

In keeping with her role in the drama Charlotte Ives Cobb Godbe penned a letter to Mrs. Hayes defending polygamy. Then six months later she delivered an aggressively feminist lecture to a large congregation in the Logan Tabernacle. Employing the same rhetoric she had used when speaking before suffrage audiences in Boston and Washington, Charlotte told the Mormons that "the rights of all as women, must be respected," and she urged women "to stand by each other, setting aside trifling differences and all work unitedly for the good of the whole."[38] Thus, Charlotte Godbe closed the first decade of Utah women's experience with the ballot with a strong feminist statement.

Notes

[1] *Salt Lake Tribune*, 7 July 1871. Together, Anthony's 1871 Diary, the *Salt Lake Tribune*, and the *Deseret News* give a picture of their stay in Salt Lake City.

[2] Elizabeth Cady Stanton, *Eighty Years and More* (New York: European Publishing, 1898), p. 284.

[3] Ibid.

[4] *Salt Lake Tribune*, 1 July 1871.

[5] Ibid.

[6] Amasa Mason Lyman Journal, 2 July 1871, Church Archives.

[7] *Salt Lake Tribune*, 7 July 1871.

[8]Stanton, *Eighty Years and More*, p. 285

[9]Lyman Journal, 16 June 1871.

[10]As quoted in *Salt Lake Tribune*, 19 July 1871. These views are discussed in Alma Lutz, *Susan B. Anthony: Rebel, Crusader, Humanitarian* (Boston: Beacon, 1959), pp. 186-87; and Harper, *Anthony*, 1:390.

[11]Ibid.

[12]*Salt Lake Herald*, 22 January 1872.

[13]George A. Smith to Colonel Lucas B. Marsh of Boston, 9 March 1872, *Journal History of the Church*.

[14]Cornelia Paddock, *The Fate of Madame La Tour* (New York: Fords, Howard, Hulbert, 1881), p. 295.

[15]*Salt Lake Tribune*, 10 February 1871.

[16]*Salt Lake Tribune*, 23 November 1871.

[17]D. A. Goddard to Henry B. Blackwell, 27 August 1872, in National American Woman Suffrage Association Records, Library of Congress Manuscript Division.

[18]*Salt Lake Tribune*, 20 February 1872.

[19]Elizabeth D. Kane, *Twelve Mormon Homes Visited In Succession On A Journey Through Utah and Arizona* (Philadelphia: Printed for private circulation by the author's father William Wood, 1874), pp. 77-78.

[20]Numerous women went to the polls and voted, or attempted to vote, in those days on the basis of citizenship.

[21]Frederick T. Frelinghuysen to Henry Wilson, 24 December 1873, as published in *Woman's Journal*, 10 January 1874.

[22]*Deseret News*, 14 February 1873.

[23]*Baltimore American*, 28 March 1888.

[24]*Woman's Journal*, 15 December 1873.

[25]*Washington Star*, 20 January 1874.

[26]1876 Report of the National Woman Suffrage Association, Manuscript Division, Library of Congress.

[27]*Woman's Journal* article as reprinted in *Deseret News*, 23 January 1874.

[28]Emmeline B. Wells to Brigham Young, 13 November 1876, Wells Papers, Church Archives.

[29]Ibid.

[30]Kirby to Woodruff, 5 February 1889.

[31]*Deseret News*, 9 May 1877.

[32]George Q. Cannon to John Taylor, 28 January 1878, Cannon Papers, Church Archives.

[33]Cannon to Taylor, 19 March 1878.

[34]*Deseret News*, 31 July 1878.

[35]*Deseret News*, 11 January 1879.

[36]Cannon to Taylor and Taylor's replies for the months of January and February 1879, Taylor Letterbooks and Cannon Papers both at the Church Archives give a picture of how the two women were received by the suffragists and how the Mormons viewed this visit as an effective maneuver against the antipolygamy movement which was making itself felt in the national capital now that the 1862 law had been declared constitutional.

[37]*Philadelphia Times*, 19 January 1879.

[38]*Salt Lake Herald*, 20 May 1879.

IV. WOMAN SUFFRAGE NULLIFIED

. . . whatever he intends, his bill is a blow at woman suffrage, and only a
fool or a knave would deny it. But it does not matter so much what a gun
is aimed at, as what it hits.

Belva A. Lockwood
Speech before NWSA
January 24, 1883

Speaking before the National Woman Suffrage Association, Belva A. Lockwood directed her sharp rhetoric at Congressman George William Cassidy of Nevada, but her critique applied generally to a number of bills then before the Forty-Seventh Congress which proposed to wage war on the institution of polygamy by disfranchising all the women of Utah. Lockwood, who, thanks to special legislation sponsored by prosuffrage Senators Sargent, Butler, and Hoar, in 1879 had become the first woman lawyer admitted to practice before the Supreme Court of the United States, was enraged because the legislation of the 1880s was taking on a new cast. Laws were passed to keep polygamists and their wives from the voting booths, yet some congressmen persisted in trying to stop all women from voting. It became more and more apparent, as Lockwood pointed out, "only a fool or a knave would deny it," these attacks were simply against the principle of woman suffrage.

In the 1880s the concept of women's equality in politics was tested on the national scene and in Utah. Before the decade closed, women in Utah would no longer be permitted to vote and the national suffrage association would be greatly weakened as a result of its identification with "the Mormon Question."

In 1880, when there were petitions in Congress to disfranchise the women of Utah and opposing petitions to "remove the political disabilities of women" by passing an amendment enfranchising all women in the nation, Charles W. Penrose, editor of the *Deseret News*, introduced a bill in the Utah territorial assembly "for the removal of the political disabilities of the women of Utah." Penrose's proposal was to strike the word "male" from the statute defining qualifications for holding office. He insisted, as he had earlier when Mary E. Cooke had been presented as a candidate for public office, that it was inconsistent to bar women from holding office simply because they were women. He went on to remind the legislators that the women of Utah participated in political conventions, selected candidates, and voted. Why then should they not be allowed to be elected to public office?

While leading Mormon women presented petitions in favor of Penrose's bill, the Mormon church president analyzed the political implications of such a measure. Arguing that certain offices might be placed at the disposal of women without much difficulty and probably with a political effect favorable to the Mormons, President John Taylor wrote to Delegate Cannon in Washington, D. C., asking his opinion of the propriety of passing this law allowing women to be elected to political office in Utah Territory. Detailing his position further, President Taylor explained:

In view of the good results, heretofore experienced from our actions in favor of woman suffrage, by the women of the nation, we might give our sisters further privileges, if our National Legislature would not take matters into their own hands, and place them in a worse position than they were before the suffrage was given, by repealing both the former law, as also that which may be passed.[1]

In his answer to Taylor's inquiry, Cannon reviewed the whole question of political privileges for women:

My views respecting the law removing the disabilities of women are very clear. The woman suffrage question and the right of women to hold office are growing in importance every day. They are the questions which politicians must meet before long. The sturdier ones are aware of this, and many of them are shaping their course accordingly. Many of them who in their hearts are opposed to this extension of privileges to women, dare not oppose the women suffragists openly, for they fear that by so doing they might lose votes. They feel that these people have too much influence for them to offend. This is more particularly the case with members from every part of the States but the South. Hence, you may have noticed that the Senate and House Judiciary Com's. allowed them [representatives of the suffrage associations] to make arguments before them; and (a mark of respect almost unprecedented) the House has ordered them to be printed.

The extension of the suffrage to our women was a most excellent measure. It brought to our aid the friends of woman suffrage, and personally I know they have been of great aid. Hon. Geo. F. Hoar (no[rthern] U. S. Senator from Mass.) helped defeat the McKee Bill in the 43rd Con. and worked cordially with me to that end, because as he told me, he is with us. Others felt as he did. Senator Sargent's friendliness was not decreased by our attitude on the suffrage of women, for his wife is one of the leaders of the movement. The women have rallied cordially to our defense because of what we have done; and they are not to be despised, for their cause is gaining ground daily. Were I at home, therefore, I would advocate the removal of political disabilities from women. The measure has more than one good effect. It shows the world that we are not afraid to trust our women — that we recognize them as our sisters, and in a certain sense our equals, and that we are willing that they shall not be handicapped in the race of life; but if there is an office which a woman is as capable of filling as a man, that she shall not be debarred from it. I would advocate the measure in full confidence that our women could be controlled, so far as office and its candidates is concerned, as the men. It would be a good stroke of policy in giving us influence and placing us in the van of this movement.

These, in brief, are my views. The governor will probably not sign the Bill; but we will have the moral effect if he should not. Should it become a law, and Congress would undertake to nullify it, they would soon have a hornet's nest about their ears, and whether they should nullify it or not, we should still get the advantage, and have a powerful element in sympathy with us.[2]

When the question was debated in the Utah territorial legislature, it became clear that in most of the men's minds women were suited to hold treasurer positions and elective offices related to education. The legislation did not limit the offices women could seek, but the intended limits were clear. Nevertheless, as Cannon had predicted, when the bill was passed by the territorial legislature, Governor George W. Emery did not sign it into law. Thus, Utah women were denied the right to hold office, and their right to vote was again under severe attack.

"Stand by your guns. Allow no encroachment upon your liberties. No mandamus here," was the message telegraphed to Emmeline B. Wells from Washington, D. C., September 28, 1880, by Belva A. Lockwood. This note of encouragement was prompted by the fact that the Supreme Court of Utah Territory was considering the constitutionality of the law giving women of the territory access to the ballot. The case had been filed by George R. Maxwell, who earlier had tried to persuade Congress to deny Delegate Cannon his seat because women had voted for Cannon. The suit, supported by the Liberals, requested the Salt Lake county registrar to remove the names of women from the registry list on the basis that different qualifications were required of women voters than of men voters: Women were not required to be taxpayers in order to vote but men were. The suit sought to have the act conferring the female franchise declared unconstitutional because the voting requirements for women were easier than those for men. After deliberation, the justices refused to order the removal of women's names from the registration list on procedural grounds, thus avoiding the question of the validity of the legislation enfranchising women. Nevertheless, in their statements the justices strengthened the idea that the legislature had the power to set different voter qualifications for different classes of citizens if it so desired. It was pointed out that such a suit would strike at the tax qualifications imposed on male voters rather than at the basic concept of women's right to vote.

Such assaults on woman suffrage by territorial liberals and national legislators tended to rally national suffragists. The National Woman Suffrage Association warned:

Let this attempt to deprive the women of Utah of their political rights, nerve the heart and soul, and fire the brain of every woman to more strenuous efforts of a sixteenth amendment which shall recognize the right of all United States citizens to the ballot. When once this is gained, no isolated State or Territory can strike such a blow at suffrage rights.[3]

While women's rights advocates were becoming more vocal defenders of Utah women's right to the ballot, antipolygamy women throughout the country were strengthening their own organizations and becoming more actively involved in congressional petitioning.

There were antipolygamy societies in Cleveland, New York, Washington, D. C., New Orleans, Sacramento, Chicago, and New England. Frequently, these anti-polygamists were aligned with the temperance workers. Especially in Ohio, there was a direct tie between the antipolygamy society and the Women's Christian Temperance Union. Supported by such eminent religious leaders as Henry Ward Beecher, Lyman Abbott, and Robert G. Ingersoll, these societies held mass meetings and gathered petitions demanding that Congress eradicate polygamy.

In Utah the antipolygamy society was led by two ex-Mormons, Sarah A. Cook and a Mrs. Chislett, and two prominent non-Mormon women — Mrs. Hollister, sister of Schulyer Colfax, who was himself delivering lectures against polygamy in Chicago, and Jennie A. Froiseth, editor of the *Antipolygamy Standard*, who had moved to Salt Lake City in 1871 to marry an army surveyor assigned to Fort Douglas. As vice president of the National Antipolygamy Society, Froiseth traveled about the country lecturing in the hope of strengthening sentiment against the peculiar Mormon marriage practice and forming branches of the society. While Froiseth and other antipolygamists were members of the National Woman Suffrage Associa-tion and were supporters of woman suffrage everywhere but in Utah, they fre-quently met and prepared petitions expressing their opposition to plural marriage and memorializing Congress to make effective the antipolygamy law of 1862. By showing that the Mormon women voted the Mormon ticket, they warned woman suffragists around the country that their cause was not being advanced in Utah.

In an effort to counter this negative publicity, Mormon church president John Taylor commissioned Charlotte Godbe to go to the nation's capital to solicit sup-port for Utah women. Charlotte met with Belva Lockwood, whom Charlotte later claimed she had persuaded to defend Utah women. In addition to discussing the problem with suffragists, Charlotte talked with the wife of outgoing President Hayes. Initially, Charlotte seemed to be the ideal person to counter the antipoly-gamy campaign. She was a feminist, yet she was a member of the church. Report-ing to John Taylor that Charlotte "passes well" in Washington society, George Q. Cannon noted that "her style, which arouses objections sometimes at home, serves a good purpose in the world." Two weeks later, however, Cannon wrote to Taylor that he had changed his opinion of Charlotte and would explain his reasons to the president in person upon his return to Salt Lake City.[4] Since Cannon was un-willing to commit his views to writing, we do not know what caused him to change his mind about Charlotte as a representative of Utah women.

About this time two other prominent Mormon women ventured East on a lec-ture tour. They, too, were concerned with improving the image of Mormon women. Widowed physician, Ellen B. Ferguson, who in 1870, prior to moving to Utah, had been a delegate representing Indiana at the first annual American Woman Suf-frage Association, and Zina D. H. Young, one of Brigham Young's wives, stopped at Buffalo, New York, to attend the Woman's Congress then went on to New England. At the Woman's Congress, an outgrowth of the American Association for the Advancement of Women headed by Julia Ward Howe, the two women were sponsored by the national suffrage leader Sarah J. Spencer of Washington, D. C. After quietly listening to the feminist rhetoric of Belva Lockwood, the two Mormon women traveled to Hartford, Connecticut, where Dr. Ferguson was a guest of Isabella Beecher Hooker.

While Dr. Ferguson and Zina Young were lecturing in the East, Senator Edmunds' bill to punish polygamists was being debated in the national Congress. Consequently, the two Mormon women considered attending the 1882 National Woman Suffrage Association convention to rally support for the Mormon cause among the women's rights advocates as had so often been done in the past. George Q. Cannon, however, telegraphed John Taylor that it would not be wise for the women to attend the convention since the leaders of the woman suffrage association were courting popularity for their cause and were becoming very defensive about their loyalty to monogamy. After discussions with suffrage leaders, particularly Jane H. Spofford, proprietor of the Riggs House where Cannon boarded while in Washington, he reported his conclusion that if the woman suffragists were pushed on the subject they would probably speak out strongly against plural marriage. Therefore, Mormons should assume a wait-and-see stance.

In spite of the fact that Mormon women refrained from attending the conference, a protest against disfranchising the women of Utah was lodged by the lawyer Phoebe Couzins.

Meanwhile, Mormon women in Utah expressed their eagerness to employ the often used strategy of agitating against hostile legislation by holding mass meetings and producing "mammoth" petitions. "Stand still," assume a "calm and serene demeanor," was Cannon's counsel to the sisters. He cautioned: "The real fighting is yet to come, and until that does come, it would not be prudent to exhaust our ammunitions or our strength." Delegate Cannon tried to convince President Taylor not to allow the Mormons to become anxious over the news dispatches from Washington. He felt it essential to wait until the congressional committees had acted on the petitions they were receiving, held hearings, and determined their course of direction before the Mormons should move. When tangible propositions were made, the Mormons could determine what the impact would be, and they could respond accordingly. Then, mass meetings and petitions could be employed with good effect; at that point, according to Cannon, they would appear to be the natural expression of intense feelings on the part of those who would be deeply and vitally affected by the proposed legislation. If applied in this manner, "eloquent remonstrances," according to the Mormon delegate, would touch many hearts.[5]

The threat from the Edmunds' proposal was taken seriously by Delegate Cannon and others. As Henry Ward Beecher's Christian Union noted, "This statute meant business." Moreover, Edmunds' bill did not provoke woman suffragists to act because it did not attempt to get at the Mormon marriage scheme through woman suffrage. This piece of legislation proposed punishing polygamists by inflicting fines and imprisonment for cohabitation and by disbarring polygamists from voting, from holding public office, and from serving on juries. The bill specified that no male cohabiting with more than one wife could vote; likewise, no woman cohabiting with a polygamist or bigamist could vote. During the congressional consideration of the bill, an amendment removing female suffrage in Utah had been discussed but voted down in the Senate. Finally, to enforce Edmunds' bill, it was proposed that a five-member electoral commission be appointed to administer voter registration. During the debates some senators, assuring their colleagues that they were not advocates of plural marriage, cautioned that denial of rights of citizenship on the basis of sexual behavior was legislation inflicting punishment without judicial process. Yet the measure continued to gain support.

When the form of the Edmunds Bill was apparent, Delegate Cannon went into action. Petitions were sent to Congress by the Utah legislative assembly, by Mormon men, by Mormon women, and by young Mormon women; all these petitions requested delaying action on Edmunds' proposal until an investigating committee could be sent to examine the state of affairs in Utah. Attempting to utilize all forces at his disposal against the bill, Cannon visited Republican senators known to be friendly to woman suffrage and made a special appeal for their support. In addition, he sought out Susan B. Anthony and Belva Lockwood of the National Woman Suffrage Association who assured him they were ready to "render all the aid in their power to fight this proposition."[6]

Nonetheless, once the Edmunds Bill became law, President Chester A. Arthur set about appointing the five-member commission to oversee elections in Utah. When it became apparent that the commission was going to be composed of lawyers, Phoebe Couzins of St. Louis applied to be appointed and Utah feminist Charlotte Ives Cobb Godbe implored the President to let two of the five commissioners be women. As the second woman well versed in "legal lore," Charlotte recommended Belva Lockwood of Washington, D. C. President Arthur, however, refused to appoint anyone who applied for the position and ended by naming five male lawyers of his own choice to be commissioners.

While the membership of the commission was being decided, Utahns made another attempt to achieve statehood. They drew up a constitution which granted the right of suffrage to every citizen over the age of twenty-one years who had been residing in the state six months. In other words, women were included in the electorate. Ultimately this effort to become a state was also rejected. But the campaign for woman suffrage continued.

The American Woman Suffrage Association staged its 1882 convention in Omaha, Nebraska, to kick off a campaign for woman suffrage legislation in that state. At the conference the example of women voting in Wyoming was lauded by the governor of that territory. Mormon delegates Emmeline B. Wells and Zina D. H. Young were courteously welcomed, with Emmeline being re-elected vice president of the Utah chapter of the association, while Utah antipolygamist Cornelia Paddock served as a member of the association's executive committee.

While unsuccessful efforts were being made to have political privileges extended to the women of New York, Oregon, Nebraska, and Massachusetts, another court case was fought in Utah attempting to annul the act enfranchising the women of the territory. Test cases were instituted in the three judicial districts of the territory. In each case, a non-Mormon woman was refused registration on the grounds that she was a woman and therefore ineligible to register to vote. The Liberal party members, who had been unsuccessful in their earlier court case and in their attempt to persuade the commissioners to exclude women from the registry list, now sought to have the territorial district courts delcare the law void on the basis that the legislative assembly had not been authorized to enfranchise women since it was never the intention of the national Congress to confer the right of suffrage upon women. The Liberals argued that the 1859 Organic Act had not granted the territorial legislature the right to expand the franchise. The opposition lawyers, however, pointed to the fact that the national Congress had repreatedly attempted to pass legislation taking the vote from women, thereby recognizing the legality of the initial act. This conclusion also was supported by the federal Supreme Court decision eight years earlier in the Minor case, which had declared that the national Constitution did not confer the vote on anyone but left the definition of the electorate to the states. The Utah district judges ended by sustaining the validity of the act of female enfranchisement, and since they sat together to compose the territorial supreme court, further appeal was futile.

As soon as the case was settled, the political parties began appealing to the women to come to the polls and cast their votes. The Mormon-dominated People's party reminded the women that it was the party which had done the most for them: The right of franchise had been granted by a legislature elected by the People's party. Moreover, as they told the women, the party had desired to go even further and extend the right of holding political office to women, but its efforts had been thwarted by the governor. In addition, the People's party was opposed to the dowry right of a widow to one-third property of her deceased husband; instead, they favored the right of women to hold and own property in their own names after marriage as before. "Hence," the People's party claimed, "everything that has been done for the women of Utah has come from the People's party, and everything oppressive to them proceeded from the 'Liberals.'"[7]

In the first annual report to the Secretary of the Interior from the Utah commission, A. S. Paddock reported that the question of abolishing woman suffrage had come before the commission, but they had felt they had no jurisdiction in the matter. However, he advised Congress that what might be said in favor of female suffrage elsewhere could not be applied in Utah since the women were completely controlled in their actions by the church authorities. Going further, the commissioners included in their report a draft of suggested amendments to the Edmunds Bill, among them a clause repealing the Utah statute which conferred voting privileges on women, which Edmunds accepted and introduced in Congress.

Woman suffragists were provoked by this new Edmunds Bill and the other similar measures such as Cassidy's legislation to "elevate" the women of Utah and "relieve" them from their "bondage" by repealing the territorial act conferring upon the women the elective franchise. Consequently, in 1883 Belva Lockwood, who said, "it is not only a fight for 'Mormon' female votes — it is a contest for woman's equal rights on principle,"[8] launched a vigorous campaign against these measures designed to annul the Utah woman suffrage statute. At the preliminary meeting the National Woman Suffrage Association held at the Riggs House prior to the convening of the annual conference, Lockwood persuaded the members to adopt a resolution condemning the legislation proposed by Cassidy. Lockwood was angry. As she told the suffragist convention, "Only a fool or a knave would deny" that Cassidy's bill was obviously a direct blow at the principle of woman suffrage. As Lockwood analyzed it, some congressmen, led by Cassidy, Edmunds, and Cullom, seemed to have their digestion disturbed over the morals of the republic as they talked continually about bigamy and polygamy; but they could no longer hide behind this cover of exalted purity and patriotism. It was now apparent that they wanted to disfranchise citizens whose only crime was being women. As Lockwood said, for no fault of their own, they were what Mr. Edmunds called "females," a term which might apply equally to a dog or a cat. She went on to say that for this crime Edmunds proposed to punish them without judge or jury, and by a fiat of law deprive 10,000 women citizens of the ballot.[9]

Lockwood's appearance as a representative of the National Woman Suffrage Association before the House Judiciary Committee, where she made similar protests against the legislation disfranchising the women of Utah, and her aggressive address before the suffragists, received the notice of Utahns. At the quarterly conference of the Ogden Relief Societies, suffrage worker Emily S. Richards, who had made Lockwood's acquaintance the previous year, read the Washington lawyer's address, after which Emily's father-in-law, Franklin D. Richards, moved a vote of thanks to attorney Lockwood. Now, Utahns laughed even less when they told the story of "plucky Mrs. Lockwood" riding down Pennsylvania Avenue on her tricycle.

In her aggressive defenses of Utah, Lockwood went further than many other suffragists were willing to go. As Delegate Cannon phrased it, many of these women were becoming "afraid to say anything favorable to women of Utah for fear that it might hurt their cause."[10] Moreover, the Utah commissioners' report and antipolygamists' descriptions of the application of woman suffrage in Utah made many suffragists wonder if they should continue to support Utah if suffrage there was really an example of women voting as they were instructed. In addition, they correctly assumed that they were being identified with polygamy. In a series of articles, the Chicago *Inter Ocean* fed these doubts by insisting that the resolution against the congressional legislation related to Utah, which had been proposed by Lockwood and adopted by the National Woman Suffrage Association, put the suffragists in "an attitude not unfriendly to polygamy."[11]

While suffragists' image was being tarnished by identification with polygamy,

Belva A. Lockwood

Cornelia Paddock and other non-Mormon women of Utah entertained Alice Stone Blackwell, daughter of Lucy Stone and Henry B. Blackwell, when she visited Utah in 1883. Upon her return to Boston Miss Blackwell prepared a number of articles for the *Woman's Journal* in which she appealed for support of the antipolygamy movement.

Acknowledging that her heart was deeply pained by the division in the woman suffrage ranks, Utah feminist Charlotte Godbe reminded Utahns that she too had a Boston heritage, and she urged women to stand together. Women, regardless of sect or party, should unite against sin and intemperance, Charlotte argued. "The era for women has dawned and in union only lies strength," she announced.

> When earnest women can strike hands of fellowship and clasp them around the world in united effort, setting aside all petty ambition and personal gain, then, and not till then, will men accept us as the power we really have it in us to be.[12]

Despite Charlotte's pleas for feminist unity, Angie Newman, superintendent of Utah work for the Home Mission Society of the Methodist church, who was supported by the Women's Christian Temperance Union, persisted in efforts to have the women of Utah disfranchised and to establish an industrial home in Salt Lake City as a place for women who wanted to abandon polygamy to earn a living and as a sort of underground railroad for all such as desired to escape from the territory.

Antipolygamy seemed to be growing in popularity. Kate Field, who had been in Salt Lake City gathering material for a book on "the Mormon Question," was invited by the Democratic national party to prepare an antipolygamy plank for its national platform. Kate, who was not herself a supporter of woman suffrage, nonetheless, expressed surprise that women would petition to take the vote from other women.

Despite the New York State Woman Suffrage Association protests and Senator Hoar's effort to have the seventh section disfranchising the women of Utah removed, the Edmunds Bill was released from committee. At the same time, Senator Cullom offered a similar bill in the Senate, Cassidy reintroduced his in the House, and Luke P. Poland, the congressman from Edmunds' home state of Vermont, introduced a bill disfranchising all Mormons in Utah and Idaho territories.

It was for these reasons that the leaders of the 1884 National Woman Suffrage Association meeting in Washington called on the President and visited the House Judiciary Committee to protest the proposals to take the vote from the women of Utah. Meanwhile, in Utah, funds were being raised by Jane Richards, Eliza R. Snow, and Emmeline B. Wells, with President Taylor's approval, "to aid in maintaining the cause of Woman's Suffrage." Ultimately, four hundred donated dollars were forwarded to the Utah delegate to Congress, John T. Caine, to be turned over to Belva Lockwood "to aid her to work for Utah's interest."[13]

Charlotte Godbe gave the following account of how it came about that money was sent to Belva Lockwood:

She [Lockwood] wrote to me a letter saying 'Get a petition signed by some of your most influential women protesting against the Suffrage being taken from you, and I will see that it is *not thrown under the table.'* I took it to a meeting in the 15th Ward, and asked the privilege of reading it. Sister Horne & a few of the sisters presiding looked at it, & then invited Zina Young, Aunt Zina's [Huntington Young] daughter to read it — it was a *Lawyer's* penmanship, & with great difficulty she made out to get at the *point* of the letter; it was then handed back to me, no comments.

Continuing, Charlotte recounted another episode in her ongoing conflict with Emmeline B. Wells.

But there was *one* who saw the *points,* she, Em[m]eline Wells, immediately set about raising money to buy my friend, & our poor sisters were called upon to donate to this fund five hundred dollars, to pay Belva, for doing that which she had offered me to do for nothing.[14]

When "Aunt Zina," as Charlotte called Brigham's wife, asked Charlotte to "work *with* the women, & throw a useful life in with theirs," Charlotte assured her that she would not join *her* efforts on behalf of women's rights with those of the Mormon women until first, Zina was "at the head of the women here," and second, "the women of Utah touch Suffrage." Then Charlotte said she would "come to the front, for that is my work."[15] It would be another five years before these circumstances would exist and Charlotte could put aside her animosity towards Emmeline B. Wells to join with the other Mormon women of Utah on behalf of woman suffrage.

In 1884 Lockwood again spoke on the constitutionality of Cassidy's bill and the amendments proposed for the 1882 Edmunds Bill. First she presented her views to the National Woman Suffrage Association, then she argued a similar case before the House Committee on Territories. In so doing, she "incidentally defended the Mormon Church," as the Salt Lake *Herald* phrased it. After Lockwood's speech, however, Susan B. Anthony made it clear that the National Woman Suffrage Association's only concern with the Utah question was that part of it which related to woman suffrage.

Alluding to these speeches and numerous other lectures Lockwood had delivered from New York to Chicago, which often dealt as well with "the Mormon Question," a reporter for the *Democrat and Chronicle* of Rochester interviewed Lockwood while she was in upstate New York. He asked her if her opposition to the proposed legislation regarding Utah was based upon the fact that she was "employed by the Mormon leaders as their attorney to look after their interests in Congress." To this she replied, "I have never been employed by the Mormons. I never have defended the institution of polygamy, and I have no defense for it; and I am not a paid attorney for these people." Explaining her position in detail, she acknowledged that for the past ten years whenever a proposal to disfranchise the women of Utah had been introduced in Congress she had appeared before the committees of both houses in an effort to defeat the measure. Moreover, she admitted she had presented legal arguments against three bills which had been before Congress the previous year all designed to take the vote from the women of Utah. Referring to these bills, she concluded: "Now, you must not make me say I defeated them, but they were defeated." On the subject of money, she reported she had had discussions early in the session of the Forty-Eighth Congress with Delegate Cannon and some Utah women about how legislation disfranchising Utah women could be blocked, and that in these discussions she had suggested that the Mormons send a delegation of women to Washington; but the idea had been abandoned after talking with Susan B. Anthony who reportedly had said to the Mormons, "Don't send women but send us money."[16] It was thus, Lockwood reported, that the Mormon women had raised funds to send to the women running the equal suffrage campaign in Washington.

In 1884 the Equal Rights party meeting in San Francisco endorsed Lockwood as their candidate for President of the United States. She campaigned with her vice presidential nominee Marietta L. B. Snow, San Francisco editor of *Women's Herald of Industry*, on a platform promising equality and justice to all, regardless of color, sex or nationality; equal voting and property rights to women; pensions for soldiers; temperance; uniform marriage and divorce laws; citizenship for Indians; expansion of commerce with foreign countries; peace; and an end to corruption in high places. Nonetheless, many prominent sufffragists such as Anthony and Stanton supported the candidacy of Republican James G. Blaine. In the same presidential campaign, Benjamin F. Butler, long-time friend of woman suffrage, was the standardbearer for the Greenback party. When the votes were tallied, ending one of the most scurrilous campaigns in American history, Lockwood polled 4,149 votes to secure last place in the race behind the Prohibition party candidate John P. St. John, the Greenbacker Butler, the Republican Blaine, and the new Democratic President — Grover Cleveland.

Lockwood conceded defeat, but asserted that the campaign had demonstrated that a woman could, constitutionally, be voted for and elected to the Presidency or either house of Congress. In their new *National Equal Rights* newspaper devoted to the advocacy of women's rights, editors Lockwood and Snow immediately announced that they would be candidates in the 1888 Presidential campaign.

During the summer after the 1884 election, Belva Lockwood spent ten days in Utah as a guest at the home of Emily S. and Franklin S. Richards while she lectured in Salt Lake City, Ogden, Logan, and Provo on "Political and Social Life in Washington" and "The Women of Today." When Lockwood left Utah she was heralded by the Mormon press as a brave, outspoken woman who had ever been a warm and consistent friend of the people of Utah. The *Tribune* editor was less friendly. Later he published a long tirade about her under the headline: "An Unsexed Monster."

Continuing her lecture tour which would take her to California and the Northwest then back East via the Northern Pacific Railroad, Lockwood took a day off for rest at the Lake Tahoe resort. However, she spent part of that day writing a long letter to President Grover Cleveland defending the Mormons. The letter, a copy of which she forwarded to Delegate Caine, was written in response to newspaper reports of the dispatch of federal troops to Utah to quell anticipated fighting between the Mormons and non-Mormons. She assured the President that no such conflict was imminent. After characterizing the Mormons as "sober, honest, industrious citizens . . . strongly attached to their religion," Lockwood reminded President Cleveland that "the *suppression of a religion* is opposed *not only to the spirit but to the wording of the constitution.*"[17]

As Lockwood devoted more of her time to lecturing and her law practice, the controversy over women in Utah continued. The Utah territorial legislature presented a bill prescribing qualifications for electors and office holders, but Governor Eli H. Murray vetoed it and listed as his objection that it reenacted woman suffrage "without expressing any opinion in the merits of woman suffrage elsewhere." In addition, he declared he doubted the constitutionality of the original law conferring woman suffrage in Utah and must therefore decline to approve any act giving it validity.

While the Utah commission repeatedly endorsed the idea of disfranchising the women of Utah as a means to suppress polygamy, the proposals to make the Edmunds law more stringent were kept in the public light by antipolygamy societies which persisted in their demand that Mormon women be disfranchised because they voted under compulsion from the church hierarchy. In 1885 supplemental suggestions were made advising the examination of the Idaho plan of disfranchising all Mormons in all territories.

Suffragists and suffragist supporters, especially Senator Hoar, continued to argue that disfranchising the women of Utah was not fair to those women of the territory who had nothing to do with polygamy; moreover, it was an unjustifiable violation of vested rights. Reverend Anna Howard Shaw summed up the objections when she described the bill as an insult to the womanhood of America.

In 1886 Anna Howard Shaw, Henry Blackwell, and Mary A. Hunt presented the arguments of the American Woman Suffrage Association before the House Committee on Territories, objecting to the proposed disfranchisement of Utah women. They also petitioned for a law to give women equal suffrage in all the territories. As justification for such a law, they pointed to the recent veto of a woman suffrage bill in Dakota by the governor of the territory and the proposed disfranchisement of Utah women.

Clemence S. Lozier, M.D., president of the New York State Woman Suffrage party, aggressively responded to a letter Senator Edmunds had written to a member of the New York association advising the suffragist that if she and her associates understood the state of affairs in Utah they would support instead of oppose the provision to relieve the women of Utah from the degradation of voting as their Mormon masters required. Edmunds justified his position further by saying the state of law was such that it was "impracticable to disenfranchise Mormon women without including the Gentile women." Dr. Lozier responded, "The woman suffragists do understand the state of things in Utah, and long have done so. Indeed, woman suffrage in Utah was originated by one of their most devoted leaders -- Mr. Hamilton Willcox . . . [who] stated in 1869 that the abolition of disfranchisement would at first strengthen polygamy, but would afterward operate to overthrow it." Arguing from a position of God-given and vested legal rights, Dr. Lozier referred to Edmunds' proposal as "a sheer attack on womanhood, an attempt to stigmatize and punish thousands of pure women for the crime of being women." Going further she warned Edmunds that his "aristocratic, tyrannical, and reactionary" behavior in this matter had destroyed his prospects for the Presidency since his party's leaders knew that he could not carry New York and "though disenfranchised, the womanhood of America" would manage to turn other states against him. Dr. Lozier did not stop once she had answered Edmunds' letter and publicized her reply. She distributed the two letters to friends of woman suffrage and requested them to send copies to John Randolph Tucker, chairman of the House Judiciary Committee, asking him to use his "utmost influence to prevent the disenfranchisement of the nonpolygamous women of Utah."[18] As the Mormon press summarized it, Edmunds' bid for the Presidency was doomed because the woman suffrage people were after him with their "sharp sticks."

Though Belva Lockwood was not leading the effort, in 1886 the National Woman Suffrage Association members again pled with congressmen not to take the vote from Utah women. Since her visit to Salt Lake City, Lockwood was working more directly with Mormon leaders. Telling Delegate Caine that she thought "a thorough discussion of the Utah Question in the House would kill the Edmund's [sic.] Amendment," Lockwood asked, "why do you not make a determined move to admit Utah as a State?" As she assured Caine, she had watched "the movements of Congress closely, — the passage of the Edmund's [sic.] Amendment by the Senate, which we staved off last year, — the attempt of the other Territories to be admitted, and the feeling in the West." Consequently, she declared she was persuaded, "There never was a more favorable opportunity than the present to agitate the question." But she cautioned: "Evidently the *polygamy part must be relinquished*, and it is better that, that portion should be conceded, before your people, men and women, are disfranchised, and the Church dispoiled [sic.]."[19]

When the suffragist support was at its height, the Mormon women again appealed for relief from attacks on polygamy. The 1886 Mormon women mass meeting and petition to the President and Congress is an example of how the familiar procedure was employed. Isabella M. Horne, Sarah M. Kimball, and Dr. Romania B. Pratt proposed in a letter to President John Taylor that the sisters hold a public protest meeting against the indignities they felt were heaped upon women in the districts' courts; in response, Taylor said he had no objections and suggested that Angus M. Cannon could probably aid the women if they would call upon him.

Copies of numerous speeches delivered by the women at the Salt Lake Theatre rally protesting the treatment women suffered from federal officials in the polygamy trials and the disfranchisement of Utah women were taken to Washington, D. C., by Emmeline B. Wells and Dr. Ellen B. Ferguson. The two women went to the nation's capital with President Taylor's blessing and consent as trustee-in-trust of the church in the form of railroad passes and an advance to pay expenses. However, when the women suggested that Dr. Romania B. Pratt also journey to the capitol, the head of the church advised them that Franklin S. Richards would probably take his wife, Emily S. Richards, with him to Washington and that would make three women in the national capital to make the Mormon cause known. While he had no objection to Dr. Pratt going if the sisters raised the money, Taylor thought "the same money might be profitably spent in sustaining those already there."[20] Praising the ninety-one page women's memorial as "an efficient one," Taylor advised Cannon and Caine that since it had been printed in the Congressional Record, they could circulate it at comparatively little cost, and its wide distribution would bring the wrongs imposed on the Mormons "to the knowledge of the people in a forcible manner." Caine was requested by Taylor to order twenty thousand reprints of the women's memorial, and the two Washington representatives were further advised that "in the South they will understand the situation through their own bitter experience with carpetbag government."[21]

When he responded to Emmeline B. Wells' report of her Eastern trip, President Taylor expressed his appreciation and noted that her interviews "with the Poet [John Greenleaf] Whittier, Lucy Stone and other prominent individuals" could not but "do good."[22] Thus ended another episode in which the women of Mormondom were used effectively to protest the federal government's way of dealing with the institution of polygamy. As had always been the case, one of the prime motives for granting Utah women the vote and continuing to have them identified with the suffrage movement was to draw off congressional attacks on polygamy.

On the whole the Forty-Ninth Congress voted against woman suffrage. The House Committee on Territories did not respond favorably to the American Woman Suffrage Association proposal to enfranchise women in all the territories. The judiciary committee acted negatively; it favorably reported the amendments to the Edmunds Bill, including the section disfranchising all the women of Utah Territory. The House supported the legislation now referred to as the Edmunds-Tucker Bill because John Randolph Tucker, a congressman from Virginia, had presented the report as chairman of the judiciary committee. In addition, the judiciary committee tabled Anthony's proposed amendment while favorably reporting an amendment forbidding polygamy. Congress rejected the antipolygamy amendment, but it did subscribe to Angie Newman's scheme for suppressing polygamy by appropriating $40,000 "to aid in the establishment of an Industrial Home in the Territory of Utah, to provide employment and means of self support for the dependent women who [would] renounce polygamy, and the children of such women of tender age."[23]

Again, New York suffragist Hamilton Willcox wrote to Emily S. Richards suggesting schemes to draw off Senator Edmunds' attacks. In January of 1887 the National Woman Suffrage Association meeting in Washington, D. C., appointed a special committee to present a memorial to President Cleveland urging him to veto the Edmunds-Tucker Bill. Acknowledging that it was a serious matter to disfranchise any class, the President assured the suffragist delegation who called upon him that he would give the memorial his careful consideration. When Congress presented him with the bill, Cleveland tried to sidestep the issue. He did not sign it nor veto it; he allowed it to become law without his signature. Thus, woman suffrage in Utah was abolished.

Lockwood, however, attempted to strike back. In the same year that she was running for President in a field of six candidates, including Benjamin Harrison who would ultimately be the winner, Belva Lockwood tried to apply the Edmunds-Tucker Act to bigamists and polygamists in Washington, D. C. Since the Edmunds-Tucker Act, like the 1882 Edmunds Bill before it, provided for the punishment of bigamists and polygamists living in a territory or other places over which the United States had exclusive jurisdiction, she argued that it held in the District of Columbia as well. Along with John W. Young, Brigham Young's son and Mormon emissary in the national capital, Lockwood worked out a scheme whereby she would "fedder out" cases of bigamy and adultery in Washington, D. C., and bring them to court. The plan was to "get hold of some prominent cases" whereby an uproar over the legislation would result. Fearless and capable Lockwood, as John W. Young referred to her, was expected also "to get some of the female societies sufficiently interested in the matter to urge the enforcing of the Edmunds law in Washington."[24] With the assistance of lady physicians of the District and the matron of the jail and through other means, Lockwood was able to identify some bigamists and file cases with the district attorney. Despite the fact that some arrests were made and some cases tried, the desired uproar over the application of the Utah law, as the Edmunds-Tucker Bill was called, in the District did not result. Moreover, the women's rights organizations were not recruited to the cause.[25]

In an additional attempt to draw attention to the Edmunds-Tucker Bill and to publicize the cause of statehood for Utah, Lockwood delivered a series of lectures on "The Mormon Question: The Other Side." Assuring her audiences that she did not believe in polygamy nor was she a convert to the Mormon faith, Lockwood attacked the Edmunds-Tucker Act for disfranchising all women in Utah regardless of their religious beliefs or family arrangements. After a recitation of Mormon virtues, feminist Lockwood concluded with a plea for statehood for Utah. As she said, if there was any substantial reason why the Fiftieth Congress should not admit Utah as a state, it was because the men had tamely submitted to the disfranchisement of their women and had entirely left them out of their proposed state constitution.[26]

Though rejected by many national suffrage women, Lockwood continued to crusade for the Mormons and was in attendance at the Committee on Territories in 1888 when arguments were presented against the proposed state constitution and ultimate statehood for Utah; the fifty-eight-year-old feminist lawyer led the laughter at humorous moments in the presentation. But Lockwood's over championing of the Mormon cause and her unimpressive 1888 campaign for the Presidency caused her estrangement from the major suffrage groups. The national suffrage leaders, who had always insisted their only cause was woman suffrage, were more and more reluctant to become involved in "the Mormon Question" in any form because their movement seemed to be discredited as a result of identification with polygamy. Certainly, some saw that Lockwood and others were using the suffrage movement to promote the Mormon cause.

As a result of this estrangement and the unsuccessful Mormon campaign which seemed futile after the passage of the Edmunds-Tucker Bill, Lockwood turned her attention more and more to the Universal Peace Union. She had time for the peace movement because her law practice continued to prosper under the management of her daughter. Belva Lockwood's last big lawsuit was the Eastern Cherokee Indians case against the United States government which resulted in the Supreme Court awarding the tribe five million dollars.

Because Lockwood had tied Mormonism and woman suffrage together passage of the Edmunds-Tucker Act had a serious impact upon the National Woman Suffrage Association which for years had indirectly supported the Mormon cause. Without a doubt efforts of suffragists and prosuffrage congressmen had been a key factor which had kept legislation like the Edmunds-Tucker Act from being passed years earlier. National suffragists were further disheartened by the fact that the Senate, by a vote of thirty-four to sixteen, had rejected the woman suffrage amendment. It would be thirty-four years before the amendment would again be debated in the Senate.

The National Association with its concept of enfranchisement by constitutional amendment was greatly weakened as a result of its being identified with the Mormons and their marital system. Belva Lockwood in her defense of the Mormons, like Victoria Woodhull before her, brought the wrath of society down on the National Association. As William L. O'Neill in his analysis of *The Rise and Fall of Feminism*, has pointed out, it was as a result of suffragist identification with Woodhull and her views on monogamy that the women's rights advocates could no longer be critical of the institution of marriage without being accused of favoring free love. The same thesis is valid when applied to Lockwood and the identification with polygamy. Though the suffragists continually insisted that they were not supporters of plural marriage even though they championed the Utah women's right to vote, the feminists' image was damaged. It was now necessary for feminists to shun all criticisms of marital and family relations and assure the world that they believed in the sanctity of monogamous marriage.

The methods and feminist philosophy of Elizabeth Cady Stanton and Susan B. Anthony were discredited after 1887; consequently, they turned their attention more and more to the international movement, and negotiations were opened with the Boston-based suffragists to merge the two United States suffrage organizations.

American feminism thus took a more conservative turn. Gradually, human rights arguments were dropped, and women's moral superiority was stressed. The states' rights approach to gaining the franchise came to dominate the movement until 1914, and feminist critiques of marriage and women's role in society were set aside as suffragists concentrated exclusively on the attainment of the ballot. Stanton and Anthony would continue to be revered as the grand old ladies of the suffrage movement for a few more years, but a new, more conservative, generation of suffragists which more closely followed the Lucy Stone states' rights approach was gradually taking over. Increasingly, Anthony turned the preparations of the annual conventions over to Rachael Foster, Mary Wright Sewell, and Jane H. Spofford. Moreover, temperance was accepted as part of the suffrage movement in spite of Stanton's protestations and Abigail Duniway's warnings that it would stimulate the liquor interests to work to defeat woman suffrage.

As the finalization of the 1890 merger of the National and American associations took place, woman suffrage in the United States was at low ebb. Only the women of Wyoming continued to hold the franchise. Utah women had lost the vote by congressional action, and Washington women had, for the second time, seen their woman suffrage law declared invalid by the territorial supreme court.

Notes

[1] Taylor to Cannon, 31 January 1880.

[2] Cannon to Taylor, 7 February 1880.

[3] *National Citizen and Ballot Box*, October 1880.

[4] Cannon to Taylor, 25 January; 11 February 1881.

[5] Cannon to Taylor, 8 January 1882.

[6] Cannon to Taylor, 14 January 1882.

[7] People's party rally as published in *Ogden Daily Herald*, 7 November 1882.

[8] *Ogden Daily Herald*, 8 January 1883.

[9] Belva A. Lockwood's speech before the National Woman Suffrage Association, 24 January 1883, as printed in *Ogden Daily Herald*, 9 June 1883.

[10] Cannon to Taylor, 30 Jaunuary 1883.

[11]*Chicago Inter Ocean*, 1 February 1883.

[12]*Salt Lake Herald*, 3 September 1883.

[13]Franklin D. Richards Journal, 9, 18, 27 February 1884, Franklin D. Richards Papers, Church Archives.

[14]Kirby to Woodruff, 5 February 1889.

[15]Kirby to Woodruff, 16 February 1889.

[16]*Rochester Democrat and Chronicle*, 12 March 1884, Anthony Papers.

[17]Belva A. Lockwood to John T. Caine, 23 July 1885, Caine Papers, Utah State Historical Society; and Belva A. Lockwood to Grover Cleveland, 23 July 1885, U. S. Department of Interior, Territorial Papers for Utah.

[18]George F. Edmunds to Clemence S. Lozier, 19 February 1886; Lozier to Edmunds, 20 March 1886, printed copies in John T. Caine papers, 1886 folder, Church Archives.

[19]Lockwood from Norfolk, Nebraska, to Caine, 14 February 1886, Caine Papers, Utah State Historical Society.

[20]John Taylor to Z. D. H. Young, M. I. Horne, and Sarah M. Kimball, 26 March 1886, Taylor Letterbooks.

[21]Taylor to Caine, 12 April 1886; Taylor to Cannon and Caine, 2 April 1886, Taylor Letterbooks.

[22]John Taylor to Emmeline B. Wells, 21 June 1886, Taylor Letterbooks.

[23]*Deseret News*, 16 October 1886.

[24]John W. Young to Wilford Woodruff, George Q. Cannon and Joseph Fielding Smith, 20 August 1887, John W. Young Papers, Church Archives.

[25]Belva A. Lockwood to John W. Young, 6, 9, 26 September 1887; Lockwood to District Attorney A. S. Worthington, John W. Young Papers.

[26]Belva Lockwood, Broadside: "The Mormon Question," copyrighted 1888, Church Archives; also see Franklin S. Richards to Wilford Woodruff and George Q. Cannon, 28 February 1888, Richards Collection, Utah State Historical Society; *Utah Inquirer*, 10 February 1888; *Deseret News*, 21 February; 20 March 1888.

V. THE VOTE RECLAIMED IN UTAH

The Ogden Herald *represents, presumably, a part of Utah. Then let it not represent the greater half of Utah, of which part I am a proud member, as a namby-pamby nonentity, a mere machine to incubate the great lords of creation. We are an entity in the great body religious and politic. And we demand our rights, the rights of culture[,] of knowledge, of suffrage, of individuality and of true womanhood! And they are ours, if we take them!*

Letter to the Editor
Salt Lake *Herald*
Dated late May 28, 1887
Signed, "Homespun"

Concealed behind her "Homespun" pseudonym, Brigham Young's daughter, Susa Young Gates, who would later become a principal suffrage leader in Utah, aggressively responded to the Ogden *Herald's* assertion that women had no business meddling in politics. She emphatically announced that some women were willing to demand their rights, and one of the rights she demanded was that of suffrage.

After holding electoral power for seventeen years, the women of Utah Territory, Mormon and non-Mormon alike, found themselves disfranchised in 1887. The questions of their right to vote had come home. With the passage of the Edmunds-Tucker Bill, the federal government returned to the territory the debate as to whether women should be granted political power in the future. The women of Utah could no longer be used by the Mormon or the non-Mormon powers to achieve their goals in Congress.

Now many women of Utah were aware that if they wanted political power it was once again up to the territorial assembly and the male citizens of the territory. Consequently, a local suffrage association was organized, and efforts were made to persuade legislators and constitutional delegates of the rightness of woman suffrage, but in so doing, the women activated antisuffragists around them.

It soon became apparent that many men in Utah who had once been counted among the supporters of woman suffrage were willing to abandon the idea when it no longer promoted polygamy or statehood. After the Edmunds-Tucker law went into effect, the Mormons followed the advice of their Washington counsel George Ticknor Curtis and made a bid for statehood with a constitution which prohibited polygamy and limited suffrage to adult men. As Curtis had told Franklin S. Richards, women should not be included in the electorate because it was "not necessary to the safety of the Mormon population"; moreover, it would "probably be inexpedient to complicate the subject with the question of woman suffrage."[1] This fifth formal bid for statehood was rejected by Congress, but the process had made it apparent that the Mormons were willing to abandon polygamy if necessary and that some Church leaders no longer considered it advantageous to have Mormon women identified with the national suffrage movement.

In spite of the fact that they were disfranchised and that woman suffrage no longer seemed to have the unanimous support of church leaders, Mormon women attempted to maintain their contacts with the national suffrage organizations. Just as Anthony and Stanton allowed the exhausted National Woman Suffrage Association to become absorbed by the American organization and subsequently focused more of their attention on the International Council of Women, the Mormon women followed.

With President Wilford Woodruff's approval, Emmeline B. Wells accepted a position on the press committee of that council, and four Mormon women—Emily S. Richards, Luella D. S. Young, Margaret Caine, and Nettie Y. Snell—attended the council's annual conference in the national capital. Conveniently, these women, with the exception of Snell, were the wives of the Mormon men who represented Utah in Washington, D. C., — Franklin S. Richards, John W. Young, and John T. Caine who was the delegate from Utah Territory. As Emmeline viewed the council, it was a good forum for Mormon women because they were officially accepted as representatives of the Mormon religious auxiliaries: Emily represented the Relief Society, Luella the Primaries, Nettie the Young Ladies Mutual Improvement Association, and Margaret was a delegate at large. President Woodruff acknowledged that he considered the council's conference to be a "very important one" where there was a possibility of the sisters "doing great good." Thus, he advised Franklin D. Richards to prepare statements for the women and to instruct them in the best means to achieve the maximum enhancement of the Mormon image.[2]

By 1888 the Mormons' relationship to the National Woman Suffrage Association was not what it had been a decade earlier. Long-time Mormon champion Belva Lockwood was no longer an active suffrage worker; she had turned her attention to independent lecturing in support of the Mormons, to her second feeble campaign for the Presidency, and more and more to the international peace movement. Moreover, the National Association was attempting to rid itself of constantly criticized radical ideas. Even Stanton's *Woman's Bible* and her view on divorce were difficult for many suffragists to tolerate. The Boston-based American suffragists, who had charged the National Association with "political impropriety" for having worked with Mormon women, were insisting that such unacceptable identifications be dropped if the two suffrage organizations were to merge.

As a result, Mormon church leaders, anticipating the annual appearance of suffragists before congressional committees, met to see if arrangements could "be made to keep them [the suffragists] from speaking against Utah and her people." To this end, John T. Caine had conversations with Susan B. Anthony in which he reported he had "made all right as was desired."[3]

Shortly afterwards when a meeting of the International Council of Women was called by the National Woman Suffrage Association to celebrate the fortieth anniversary of the first women's rights convention at Seneca Falls, Mormon leaders were again afraid the suffragists would speak against them. Trying to prevent this, Wilford Woodruff wrote Joseph F. Smith who, along with John T. Caine and Franklin S. Richards, was representing the church in the national capital in efforts to have the constitution accepted. The church president said, "We hope you will be able to get along with the Woman's International Council without having any tirade against us. Your proposal to aid them is a good one and we hope you will be able to carry it out and to check any such ebullition as is threatened."[4] Details of the proposal designed to keep the Council of Women from venting their views on Mormons are not available, but part of the proposal must have included money, for Caine and Richards' wives were listed among the eleven people who donated one hundred dollars each to the organization in 1888.

In spite of strained relations between Mormons and women's rights leaders, suffragists continued to visit Utah. In the summer of 1888 Julia Ward Howe lectured on polite society in the Salt Lake City Congregational Church. In addition, Elizabeth Lyle Saxon and Clara Bewick Colby, editor of the National Woman Suffrage Association newspaper, the *Woman's Tribune,* stopped in the city on their return from a lecture tour in the Northwest where Washington's territorial supreme court, for the second time, had pronounced their woman suffrage law unconstitutional. While in Utah, Saxon and Colby reported on the International Council of Women meeting to a gathering of women at the Assembly Hall and solicited dollar subscriptions to the *Woman's Tribune.*

The same year Emily S. Richards approached the Mormon church officials with a proposal to form a Utah woman suffrage association to be affiliated with the National Woman Suffrage Association. Since the aggressive antipolygamist Jennie Froiseth was the vice president from Utah to the National Association but refused to aid or sanction Emily's organizational scheme "because she did not think woman suffrage good for Utah,"[5] Emily had to obtain special authorization from the Eastern suffrage association in order to form a territorial auxiliary. Insisting that prior to the Edmunds-Tucker Bill a territorial association had not been necessary because the women had the vote, Emily Richards persisted in her efforts, saying such an organization was needed now.

On January 2, 1889, the apostles of the church met with representatives of the Relief Society at the church historian's office to lay out a plan for the creation of a territorial woman suffrage association. In attendance at the meeting were Wilford Woodruff, Franklin D. Richards, Brigham Young, Jr., John Henry Smith, Heber J. Grant, L. John Nuttall, Zina D. H. Young, Jane S. Richards, Bathsheba W. Smith, Sarah M. Kimball, Emmeline B. Wells, and Emily S. Richards.[6] Once the gathering at the historian's office had decided that the women should proceed to organize a territorial suffrage association and possibly send one or more delegates to the annual National Woman Suffrage Association conference, President Woodruff suggested that Emily S. Richards be sent as delegate, if anyone went. He said, she was the best choice because she was "posted in these matters and had previously reported the Labors of the Ladies of this Territory at Washington."[7]

Emily S. Richards and Sarah Kimball (seated)

Although they were invited, few non-Mormon women attended the organizing meeting where Margaret T. Caine, wife of Utah's delegate to Congress, was named president of the Utah Territory Woman Suffrage Association in an uncontested election. The corresponding secretary position was filled by long-time feminist Charlotte Ives Cobb Godbe Kirby, who had created somewhat of a sensation five years earlier by marrying a wealthy Gentile mining man many years younger than she was. In her speech at the organizing meeting of the suffrage association Charlotte stressed the importance of working for woman suffrage "and instanced the great advancement which had been made in the same direction in Great Britain and on the continent of Europe, where," she reported, somewhat mistakenly, "woman's suffrage had worked with good results."[8]

In a long letter to Wilford Woodruff in which she recounted her years of suffrage work and her ongoing conflict with Emmeline B. Wells, Charlotte wrote:

A movement is now made, for a W.[oman] S.[uffrage] A.[ssociation] of Utah, I have been invited to join and while *I do not wish* to be a General, I would like some respect shown me, as the first woman, who spoke for W.[oman] S.[uffrage] for Utah, & as an earnest worker in this cause for several years, & the *di*sability—*Mrs*. E. B. W. tried to show ten years ago [a reference to the fact that she was not a polygamous wife], *now* forms my *ability* in working for this cause.

Once her own role in the new organization was made clear, Charlotte went on to the advise the church president:

We are now trying, to form a political associaton for women entirely free from religious ties into which the Methodist & Catholic woman can come & work; while holding her own consciencious [*sic.*] views. The women of other religions are not willing to admit or work with women as officers who are in any way connected with polygamy. Hence some of the best workers will have to be left out publicly, but if they will uphold the hands of those who *can* work. One year, will show God's providence in this as in all his Works.[9]

Women involved in polygamous arrangements would not be involved in the new organization; when the final slate of officers of the new association was made known, Emmeline B. Wells, Zina D. H. Young, and other plural wives were conspicuously absent. Though most of the officers were Mormons, they were participants in monogamous marriages.

As corresponding secretary, Charlotte wrote numerous letters to the local and Eastern newspapers reporting suffrage activities in Utah and generally arguing for wider acceptance of the idea. On one occasion she wrote to the editor of the Salt Lake *Herald*, saying she did not "understand why the question of sex should prevent the full and free expression of intelligence."[10]

Though, as we have seen, she was not accepted by Mormon women as one of them, Charlotte maintained her contact with the suffrage movement and was

Charlotte Ives Cobb Godbe Kirby

Emmeline B. Wells

almost always on hand when an Eastern suffragist was visiting in Salt Lake City. When the "Queen of the lecture bureau," suffragist and one-time editor of the *Woman's Journal*, Mary A. Livermore, planned to visit Salt Lake City in 1889, she contacted her acquaintance Charlotte Ives Cobb Godbe Kirby to arrange a lecture hall for her. Two decades earlier in the 1870's, when women had first been enfranchised in Utah, Charlotte had delivered a number of feminist lectures in the East; while in Boston she had stayed at the home of Mary Livermore, whom Charlotte credited with arousing her first enthusiasm concerning the subject of temperance. Charlotte now used the occasion of the Boston woman's visit to Utah to proclaim the "dawning of a woman's era," and once again she issued a call for "the women of the planet [to] join hands and encompass it."[11]

Like the other women lecturers who visited Utah in 1889, Livermore was more interested in temperance than suffrage. In the autumn three officers of the Association for the Advancement of Women—Henrietta L. T. Wolcott, E. Howland, and Antoinette Brown Blackwell—addressed a large audience in the Opera House on temperance and the historical development of the women's right movement.

After the formation of the Utah Territory Woman Suffrage Association, county chapters were created. In Ogden, Provo, Payson, Beaver City, Spanish Fork, Springville, American Fork, and other Mormon communities, women gathered, usually at the Mormon meeting house, organized a local suffrage chapter, and paid twenty-five cents membership dues. Within four months there were fourteen auxiliary societies in the territory. In many ways, however, these suffrage associations were merely another auxiliary organization of the Mormon church. As had been the case since the initial enfranchisement of Utah women in 1870, when Bathsheba W. Smith had been appointed to a mission to preach retrenchment and women's rights, women who were approved as delegates to Eastern suffrage conventions were officially set apart under the hands of the male priesthood. In addition, the church president usually appropriated funds to defray their expenses; while an apostle frequently prepared speeches for them to deliver at the national meetings. Moreover, local suffrage meetings followed the same format as the Relief Society meetings and were often held consecutively. The suffrage association, like the other women's auxiliaries, conducted a meeting in conjunction with the general conference of the church.

Though the second article of the territorial suffrage association by-laws specified its purpose was "to labor for the enfranchisement of women, regardless of party, sect, or creed,"[12] the membership was almost exclusively Mormon. Most non-Mormon women who professed a belief in woman suffrage persisted in the opinion that it was not appropriate for Utah so long as polygamy existed.

Nevertheless, there was some cooperation between Mormon and non-Mormon women. For example, they worked together to prepare exhibits for the Woman's Building at the 1893 Chicago World's Fair. Yet it was the silver question which motivated the two groups of women to their greatest display of solidarity. The theatre in Salt Lake City, on July 26, 1893, was the scene of a women's mass meeting where plural wife Emmeline B. Wells conducted the meeting while antipolygamist Jennie Froiseth spoke. Ultimately the women petitioned Congress to adopt measures "to increase the use of silver as money and enhance the price of silver bullion."[13]

In 1894, when Utah's entry into the nation was once again being discussed, the Salt Lake *Herald* editorialized that it was not "an opportune time for pressing the claims of women to the elective franchise in Utah." On the other hand, Susan B. Anthony advised that "the time to establish justice and equality to all the people" was in the formative period when the constitution was being established, and she warned the women of Utah not to be cajoled into believing otherwise. She observed that Colorado men were the only ones who had ever voted the word "male" out of their state constitution. Once admitted into the organic law, "male" was there to stay. "No, No!" she admonished, "Don't be deluded by any specious reasoning." In a clear, emphatic manner, she told the women not to be persuaded by "now is not the time" arguments such as the *Herald* was suggesting nor to allow a separate vote on the question. Women should settle for nothing short of a suffrage clause defining the electorate as "every citizen of the age of 21."[14]

At the same time, Jane Ellen Foster, president of the National League of Republican Women, addressing a Tabernacle audience on the subjects of woman suffrage and temperance, wondered outloud if Utahns in writing their constitution, would be "large enough and strong enough to put in the emancipation of women."[15]

While Eastern suffragists were watching the constitution making in Utah, sixty-six-year-old Emmeline B. Wells, who had once again emerged as the suffrage leader and was now president of Utah Territory Woman Suffrage Association, sought to capitalize on this concern to improve the image of Mormon women. When she beseeched the church president for his blessing and financial support to travel to the suffrage convention, she reminded him that Mormons had "gained considerable ground through this source," and she was sure more "good seed" could be planted which might ulitmately "bear fruit." At the very least, she thought there was the possibility of removing "prejudice from the minds of those who would listen attentively and with interest to a 'Mormon' woman, but would not think of hearing an Elder preach the same truths."[16]

"Money power" was what Emmeline told George Q. Cannon was needed when she tried to persuade him to help convince the brethren to financially support the National Council of Women. As Emmeline presented the argument, Mormon women could improve their image by participation in the Council, and they could improve themselves. For as she told Cannon, attending the Council meetings was an educational opportunity equal to "taking a college course for three months at least."[17]

Before she departed for Atlanta, Georgia, to cast Utah's fifteen votes at the 1895 National American Woman Suffrage Association convention, then on to the national capital to meet with the National Council of Women, Emmeline revealed her strategy for the inclusion of a woman suffrage clause in the state constitution in a long, confidential letter to the president of the Beaver county suffrage organization. Emmeline cautioned that neither the public nor the members of the suffrage association should know she was taking counsel from the church leaders because objections to union of church and state were being heard, even from within the suffrage association. Moreover, she warned that control of the suffrage organization should not be allowed to fall into the hands of certain "unwise women" who "were very able and members of the Church," but who might push the association to extremes and thus antagonize the opposition. According to Emmeline, the advice of the presidency and leaders of both major political parties was "to be quiet [on the subject of women suffrage] until the time comes." If the women refrained from aligning with either party and did not provoke the "whiskey element" with too much noise about prohibition, then an equal suffrage constitution could be written. In other words, as she headed east, the advice Emmeline Wells left with the president of the local suffrage chapters was to quietly watch the proceedings of the constitutional convention and attempt to convert individual delegates.[18]

Immediately upon her return from her six-week eastern junket, Emmeline issued a call for "all presidents of Women's Clubs" throughout the territory to meet with the Utah Territory Woman Suffrage Association on Monday morning, March 18, 1895, in the Probate Courtroom of the Salt Lake City and County Building. The time for quiet persuasion and polite socials had passed. It was time to memorialize the constitutional convention on behalf of women's rights.

In their equal suffrage petitions, the women from the various counties reminded the delegates that the two recently organized territorial political parties—Democrat and Republican—had with equal unanimity said that women shall be accorded equal rights and privileges of citizenship.[19] The women also invoked liberal tradition arguments of consent of the governed and tyranny of taxation without representation. Claiming to represent "the great majority of the women of Utah," the petitioners declared "the time clock of American destiny" had struck "the hour to inaugurate a larger and truer civil life." One day so many women crowded into the hall to deliver a petition that they occupied all the guest seats and even occupied the chair of an absent delegate, provoking Heber Wells to suggest that an outdoor session be held. Finally, the women appealed to the delegates' historical consciousness saying:

> The future writers of Utah history will immortalize the names of those men who, in this Constitutional Convention, defying the injustice and prejudice of the past, strike off the bonds that have heretofore enthralled woman, and open the doors that will usher her into free and full emancipation.[20]

From the onset, the convention delegates manifested strong sentiments in favor of equal suffrage. A majority of the constitutional committee on elections and suffrage proclaimed the door open to women with their proposal that the right of citizens "to vote and hold office not be denied or abridged on the account of sex." Five of the fifteen men on the committee, however, were not persuaded by the women's petitions, by speeches made before them by Mormon women, nor by a Wyoming woman's testimony that "the claim that woman was a purifying element in politics had been proven justifiable in the state from which she came."[21] A minority report was presented by Richard Mackintosh, a Park City mining company owner and Republican representing Salt Lake county, and Frederick J. Kiesel, an Ogden businessman; both were non-Mormons and ex-Liberal party members. The third member of the minority committee was a Republican from Weber county, a Mormon by the name of Robert McFarland. In their report the three recommended that the suffrage of women be kept out of the constitution and left instead to the state legislature. They expressed their concern that if the Mormon women were allowed to vote the "equality of the parties" would be destroyed, and as they said, perhaps those who had ruled before would be tempted to resume their sway. Similar arguments that woman suffrage would defeat statehood appeared on the editorial page of the Salt Lake *Tribune*.

The principal figure attempting to block the inclusion of woman suffrage in the constitution was the delegate from Davis county—Brigham Henry Roberts. In an hour-long speech before the convention, which friends and foes of women suffrage praised for its eloquence, the Mormon apostle and historian Roberts declared his disappointment with the minority report, yet he insisted enfranchishing women was inexpedient at that time. He argued that on the basis of the woman suffrage provision, Easterners opposed to Utah statehood might be able to pressure President Cleveland, who was generally not believed to be a friend of woman suffrage, to withhold his approval of the constitution. In short, Roberts thought enfranchising women would endanger statehood. As he saw it, "Statehood was wanted first of all. He would even swallow women suffrage to get it."[22]

Immediately, the friends of equal suffrage rallied to rebut Roberts' speech. While rumors flourished that antisuffragists and antiprohibitionists were collecting data and "preparing to pool issues with a view to keeping both questions out of the Convention,"[23] citizens prepared petitions favoring equal suffrage and presented them to the convention. Working from within the convention, delegates led by Franklin S. Richards, husband of suffrage organizer Emily S. Richards and son of early suffrage leader Jane S. Richards, and John F. Chidester, chairman of the committee on elections and suffrage, set out to counter the arguments of the gentleman from Davis county.

The debate continued for two weeks.[24] While inherent right and moral superiority arguments supporting the enfranchisement of women were reviewed, Chairman Chidester reminded the delegates of their party pledges, and he denied that an equal suffrage clause would cause the loss of a single vote of approval of the whole document. Quoting Jefferson, Lincoln, DeTouqueville, and Lester Ward to back his case, Franklin S. Richards argued that a "true theory of government"could only be inaugurated if equal suffrage was incorporated into organic law.[25]

As he declared the success of the movement for woman suffrage a "foregone conclusion," Mormon historian Orson F. Whitney, who had been persuaded by Richards to address the convention, received "uproarious laughter and applause" when he compared his fellow Democrat, Roberts, to the bull who stood in front of a train attempting to prevent it from passing and thus provoked the following from the farmer: "I admire your courage, but d--n your judgement." Whitney went on to insist that "it is woman's destiny to have a voice in the affairs of government. She was designed for it. She has a right to it." In conclusion, he cautioned the delegates that if they failed to act favorably upon this proposition, some future convention would so act and would, gazing upon their record with reproach, "crown her brows with the glory we have denied."[26]

While the delegates were debating the rightness verses the inexpediency of enfranchising women, the Mormon hierarchy was agonizing over the split in Mormon ranks. Initially, critics accused the church of deliberately pitting Richards and Whitney against Roberts. But the conflict was real. In a meeting of the presidency, John W. Taylor emphsized that an apostle had "no right to join any political party, or do anything else of a grave character, without first consulting the Presidency." Thus, Roberts had betrayed the church and had "broken his covenants, and should be called to account." When Wilford Woodruff "said he feared the Constitution would be defeated if Woman's Suffrage was not a part of it," Joseph F. Smith concurred and concluded that in his opinion B. H. Roberts had done more to injure the Mormons in two weeks than ten liberals had done in fifteen years. Despite these strong statements, there was not a consensus among the church leaders. George Q. Cannon and John Teasdale, for example, were in favor of omitting woman suffrage from the constitution. After considerable discussion "the result," Abraham H. Cannon recorded, "was a lack of union on the subject, and hence the matter was left for the members to do as they desired."[27]

Meanwhile, the debate continued in the convention. One of Roberts' fellow delegates from Davis county, a Mr. Barnes, read from a letter to Roberts from the chairman and secretary of that county's Democratic committee. In the letter the party officers reminded Roberts that the convention which had nominated him also had adopted a woman suffrage plank; consequently, they advised that if he could not support it, then he might at least remain silent.

Disregarding this reprimand, Roberts continued his campaign with renewed vigor. In his third and final speech before the convention in summarizing the propositions upon which he based his objections to woman suffrage, Roberts shifted from his argument that woman suffrage would endanger statehood to more traditional antifeminist statements which included the following: Due to the relationship within a family, a woman cannot act independently. The elective franchise is a privilege conferred by the state, not a right to be demanded. Finally, women are sufficiently represented in politics by husbands, fathers, sons, or brothers. When confronted with the principle of no taxation without representation, he acknowledged he would accept the enfranchisement of unmarried property holders.

Continuing, he declared "all change is not progress," and expressed the conservative theory when he said he saw no reason to change the system now if statesmen had not seen fit to grant women the ballot in the past two hundred years. He made it clear that he would not respond to the theory that women would use the ballot to reform the world until it was made clear to him just which laws they would change.[28]

As a result of this "manly stand," as Utah Commissioner William McKay described it, Roberts was a hero in some circles. In recognition of his efforts against woman suffrage, he received bouquets of roses from anonymous admirers and members' privileges for thirty days at the all male Salt Lake Alta Club. He also was in great demand as a public speaker. On one occasion his persuasive arguments led an Exposition Building audience of 500 people to adopt a resolution calling for the constitutional convention to submit the woman suffrage question to the electorate as an article separate from the constitution.

At this point, many organizations, including the Salt Lake City Chamber of Commerce, endorsed the idea of separate submission. In response to the *Tribune's* call for more petitions for separate submission, nearly a thousand women met at the Grand Opera House and signed their names to such a memorial to the convention. The speakers included Charlotte Godbe Kirby, Jennie Froiseth, and Cornelia Paddock. Roberts, of course, was also on hand at this meeting to recite his reasons for keeping a woman suffrage clause out of the constitution. After his remarks, Charlotte Godbe Kirby took issue with his view that women could not be kept sacred if "drug" into the arena of politics; but "she was also of the opinion that Mormon women would vote in the interest of women." In spite of her strong feminist stand, she was in favor of separate submission.[29] As she had said earlier, "Whatever may await us in the future, it would be suicidal to embody as a plank in the platform of our new State woman's suffrage."[30] She admitted that she was convinced that the decision on women's access to the ballot should be postponed until after statehood.

When the discussion on the convention floor turned from the merits of enfranchising women to a debate over separate submission, the delegate from San Juan declared he had endured enough pain; "he had kept his seat waiting for the end about long enough." As far as he was concerned, "the Convention had been playing to the galleries and the gods long enough."[31] Both sides, nevertheless, continued the debate a little longer. However, before adjourning for the Arbor Day weekend, they rejected the idea of a separate submission and voted seventy-five to fourteen in favor of Franklin S. Richards' motion to adopt the equal suffrage clause as submitted by the elections and suffrage committee.[32] In the final vote, Roberts voted no, while two of the minority opinion advocates—Mackintosh and Kiesel—refused to vote, and their Mormon friend, McFarland, cast his lot with the ayes.

After the convention had rendered its opinion, petitions on both sides of the question continued to arrive. As Chairman Chidester summarized it, "the opponents of equal rights for the fair sex have been protesting by tens, twenties and fifties against the Convention's action, while it is being commended by hundreds and thousands."[33] Nevertheless, there was talk "that efforts were being made to resuscitate the old Liberal party in order to defeat Statehood because of Woman's Suffrage being a part of the Constitution," and there were rumors that prohibition would be used by the Liberals to combine the saloon element against statehood. In addition, wealthy Ogden businessman and minority opinion delegate, Fred J. Kiesel, reportedly swore "he would use his money and time to defeat the Woman's Suffrage if made a part of the Constitution."[34]

Faced with the possibility of a return to the old party divisions along Mormon—non-Mormon lines, President Woodruff concluded "it would be wise to leave this provision out of the Constitution." Joseph F. Smith, nonetheless, persisted saying, "he would rather see Utah remain a territory than to see it become a State without Woman's Suffrage being a part of the Constitution."[35]

In the midst of these threats and wavering commitments, the constitutional convention reconsidered the question of woman suffrage. On April 18, by a vote of two to one, it decided to retain the equal suffrage clause in the constitution.[36] Subsequently, the grateful women of Salt Lake City expressed their appreciation by entertaining the delegates at a reception.

Eastern suffragists had watched Utah's constitution writing with great interest. Hamilton Willcox was concerned with events in Utah as he had been for over a quarter of a century. Consequently, he wrote to John T. Caine suggesting propositions to be incorporated into the new constitution.[37] When the convention debate had been at its high point, Emmeline B. Wells had announced the anticipated May 13 arrival in the territory of Susan B. Anthony and Anna Howard Shaw to conduct a woman suffrage conference. Anthony and Shaw arrived in Salt Lake City, as planned, by train in the early hours of the morning, but they remained in their sleeping cars. At seven a.m. a delegation of over fifty women, headed by Emmeline Wells, arrived to escort them to the Hotel Templeton for a Sunday breakfast followed by a tour of the city in a thirty-seat omnibus. Both women observed changes in the city since their last visits: Anthony had visited twenty-five years earlier right after the enfranchisement of the women of Utah, and Shaw had lectured in Salt Lake City just before the Edmunds-Tucker Bill had disfranchised them.

Sunday afternoon the two suffragists, along with a number of Mormon women active in the movement, were honored guests at the religious meeting where Reverend Shaw donned her cleric robes to preach a brief sermon to a gathering of over 6,000 persons which she proclaimed her largest audience ever. Anthony congratulated the people of Utah "on the fact that in the Constitution they had shown a sense of justice and generosity to the women of Utah," and wished them "the highest success in conducting the affairs of the new State." Then O. F. Whitney, who had earned a reputation as an advocate of women's rights, followed with some remarks on Mormon doctrine, concluding with the thought that the "emancipation of women was in line with the mark of progress." After meeting with the Mormons, Anthony and Shaw joined representatives of the other religious

Susan B. Anthony, 1896

Anna Howard Shaw

denominations in a "union meeting."[38]

On Monday morning a three-day Rocky Mountain Suffrage Conference convened in the flag-draped convention hall of the city and county building where the decorations from the constitutional convention, still in place, were enlivened with portraits of Stanton and Anthony hung by Lincoln's to lend a women's rights flavor. By the time Governor Caleb W. West and Emily S. Richard rose to introduce the guests, the room was, as Anthony said, "crowded to suffocation"; so it was decided that future meetings would be held in the Mormon assembly hall. Suffrage leaders from Wyoming, Estelle Kesl and Theresa A. Jenkins, and from Colorado, Mary Carroll Craig Bradford and Ellis Meredith Stansbury, were also in attendance at this celebration of woman suffrage in the "Land of the Divide." During their addresses to the conference all speakers made asides about "Hero Roberts' " behavior during the constitutional convention. Anna Howard Shaw reported that Mormon women had persuaded her to challenge Roberts to a debate on woman suffrage, but he had refused saying, "he was not willing to lower himself to the intellectual plane of a woman."[39]

During their free time the suffragists were entertained with a visit to the lakeside resort of Saltair, a reception at the home of Emily S. and Franklin S. Richards, and a social sponsored by the Women's Christian Temperance Union. In addition, they journeyed to Ogden for a banquet as guests of the Richards families and more lectures to overflow crowds in the second ward meetinghouse. Even after the suffrage women left the territory, a lively discussion continued on the subject of women's proper role in politics.

At the 1895 church quarterly conference, Abraham H. Cannon urged moderation in politics and asked "the sisters not to be foolish in exercising the franchise."[40] However, the Democrats' selection of a number of prominent church women to take part in their party proceedings gave substance to non-Mormon fears that the church intended to use the women to accomplish the things they desired "in a political way." Consequently, the presidency met to decide if they should make it policy that women should be asked to resign their church offices or to "cease mixing in politics" as Angus Cannon had already done in his stake. John T. Caine, who was leading the discussion, "expressed the fear that the withdrawal of the prominent women from the political field . . . would cause the church and some individuals trouble." After considerable discussion, President Woodruff concluded it would be best if leading women, and men, kept out of active politics. He said, he regretted the course the sisters had taken, but since they had gone so far, it was best to let them finish their campaign as they thought best. Another member of the presidency, however, insisted the women "must not use their religious meetings to promote their political cause"; moreover, they should be restrained from declaring the politics of deceased religious leaders but should instead teach the doctrines of their respective parties. But not in religious meetings![41] Partisan politics had come of age in Utah; consequently, Mormon women could no longer combine Relief Society, woman suffrage, and party politics under the same umbrella.

ROCKY MOUNTAIN SUFFRAGE CONFERENCE
May 13-15, 1895

Susan B. Anthony—front row, third from right
Margaret N. Caine—front row, first on right
Anna Howard Shaw—second row, fifth from right
Sarah M. Kimball—second row, fourth from right
Emmeline B. Wells—second row, third from right
Zina D. H. Young—second row, second from right
Mattie Hughes Cannon—back row, first on left
Emily S. Richards—back row, fourth from left
Ellis Meredith Stansbury—back row, fifth from left
Mary C.C. Bradford—third row, first on right
Theresa A. Jenkins—fourth row, third from right
Estelle Kesl—third row, third from right

Church officials were not simply concerned that prominent Mormon women who were religious and suffrage leaders were becoming actively involved in the women's leagues of the two political parties. Emmeline B. Wells had aligned herself with the Republicans, while Dr. Martha Hughes Cannon, Dr. Ellen Ferguson, Emily S. Richards, Margaret Caine, and Dr. Romania Pratt had joined the Democrats. Rather, the major concern was that some of the women were insisting, on the basis of the enabling act and the proposed constitution, that they were entitled to register and vote on the adoption of the constitution and selection of state officials.

Seeing statehood so close, many men counseled women to wait. The women were often advised to "stand back" on this election, and then, as soon as statehood was a reality, they could have the equality which so concerned them. Besides, some men warned, it was going to be "a very hot campaign"; it would be better for the women to be free of the turmoil and bitterness which would ensue. Boston suffrage leader Henry Blackwell also took a cautious stand when he wrote to Zina D. H. Young advising the women of Utah not to endanger statehood by voting in the upcoming election. Church leaders, expressing the fear that statehood would be jeopardized if women voted, decided they "would use a quiet influence to prevent the voting of women."[42]

However, Sarah E. Anderson of Ogden had brought a test case in the courts to have the problem resolved legally. When the district court ruled in favor of women participating in the election, the case was immediately appealed to the territorial supreme court where the chief justice and one of the other two judges reversed the decision of the lower court. The question was settled when the higher court ruled that it was only the state constitution which enfranchised women; thus they could not vote until it had been offically adopted.[43]

At the Farmington quarterly conference of the Mormon church, Abraham H. Cannon expressed his pleasure that women would not be allowed to participate in the autumn election, "because of the fear that their doing so may injure the chances of statehood." Moreover, he cautioned it would be "better for them to have time to study the principles of the two parties before aligning themselves with either."[44]

The court ruling that women could not vote on the adoption of the constitution also resulted in the removal of women's names from the ballots. The Republicans had nominated non-Mormon suffragist Emma J. McVicker for superintendent of public instruction, but now they replaced her name with that of John R. Park, who ultimately won the election. Lillie R. Pardee and Emmeline B. Wells also were no longer Republican candidates for the state senate and a lower house seat. Likewise, the Democrats told Dr. Martha Hughes Cannon she would have to wait a year to run for the state senate, a contest which she would enter and win in 1896. Even though they were not allowed to participate in the election as candidates or electors, many women continued their work in the campaign by organizing parades and receptions and generally working for the two parties through their separate women's organizations. There was even a separate women's Afro-American Republican Club.

Ultimately, the constitution was approved by the male electorate despite the fact that nearly one-fifth of those voting said no to the constitution and more than one-sixth of the registered voters did not vote.[45] Still an absolute majority, sixty-seven percent of all voters, voted for the constitution.

In spite of the concern in the territory, when the constitution was submitted to the national Congress for review, there was little protest over the enfranchisement of women, and President Cleveland paid no attention to the question when he issued the proclamation admitting the territory of Utah as a state of the union on January 4, 1896.

Within three weeks of Utah statehood, the National American Woman Suffrage Association conventioneers were in the national capital celebrating the addition of the third star to the suffrage flag. Anna Howard Shaw welcomed the Utah delegates, and Emily S. Richards and Sarah A. Boyer responded on behalf of the women of Utah reporting that they were happy to once again have the right to vote.

Notes

[1]George Ticknor Curtis to Franklin S. Richards, 23 January 1887, Franklin S. Richards Papers, Church Archives.

[2]Wilford Woodruff to Franklin D. Richards, 13 March 1888, Wilford Woodruff Papers; also see, Franklin D. Richards Journal, 12, 13, 16, 20 March 1888, Church Archives.

[3]L. John Nuttall Journal, 18, 19 March 1888, Church Archives.

[4]Wilford Woodruff to Joseph F. Smith, 5 April 1888, Woodruff Letterbooks.

[5]*Deseret News*, 6 Februrary 1889.

[6]These women had been and would continue to be the principal women in the Mormon community holding the major offices in both the Relief Society and the suffrage organization. The other Mormon women consistently active in the suffrage campaign were Dr. Ellen B. Ferguson, Dr. Romania B. Pratt, and Margaret Caine.

[7]L. John Nuttall Journal, 2 January 1889; also see 14 November; 31 December 1888; Franklin D. Richards Journal, 2, 10, 24 January 1889; Wilford Woodruff to "Jason Mack" [Joseph Fielding Smith], 8 January 1889, Woodruff Letterbooks.

[8]*Deseret News*, 11 January 1889.

⁹Kirby to Woodruff, 5 February 1889; also see Emmeline B. Wells Diaries, 8 January 1889, Brigham Young University Library Archives, Provo, Utah.

¹⁰*Salt Lake Herald*, 17 February 1889; also see Woodruff to Kirby, 11 February 1889, Woodruff Letterbooks.

¹¹*Salt Lake Herald*, 12 April 1889; also see Kirby to Woodruff, 5 February; 27 March 1889; and Woodruff to Kirby, 27 May 1889.

¹²Beaver County Woman Suffrage Association file, Brigham Young University Library Archives.

¹³*Deseret News*, 27 July 1893.

¹⁴*Salt Lake Tribune*, 27 July 1894.

¹⁵Copy of Jane Ellen Foster's 26 August 1894, speech in Emma Smith Woodruff [Mrs. Wilford] file folder No. 33, Church Archives.

¹⁶Emmeline B. Wells to Joseph Fielding Smith, 13 February 1894, Wells Papers.

¹⁷Emmeline B. Wells to George Q. Cannon, 25 February 1895, Wells Papers.

¹⁸Emmeline B. Wells to Mary A. White, president of the Beaver County Woman Suffrage Association, 14 January 1895, Beaver County Woman Suffrage Association Papers.

¹⁹The Utah Populist party, which included a number of the original Godbeite reformers, notably Henry W. Lawrence and William S. Godbe, had also come out for equal suffrage in that they endorsed the national party platform which advocated woman suffrage.

²⁰*Deseret News*, 20 March 1895.

²¹*Deseret News*, 19 March 1895.

²²*Deseret News*, 5 April 1895.

²³*Deseret News*, 25 March 1895.

²⁴The offical record of the constitutional convention was published in *Constitutional Convention: Offical Report of the Proceedings and Debates*, 2 vols. (Salt Lake City: Star Printing Company, 1898). An analysis of the conference debate has been done by Jean Bickmore White in her Charles Redd Lecture, published as a monograph and as "The Struggle for Equal Rights," *Utah Historical Quarterly* 42 (Fall 1974): 344-69.

²⁵Franklin S. Richards Speech, 28 March 1895, "The Suffrage Question" (Salt Lake City: Utah Woman Suffrage Association, 1895).

²⁶O. F. Whitney speech, 30 March 1895, *Men and Woman* 1 (May 14, 1895): 10-12.

[27]Abraham H. Cannon Journal, 4 April 1895; also see 28, 30 March; 23 April 1895, Utah State Historical Society; and Franklin D. Richards Journal 4, 7 April 1895, Church Archives.

[28]Brigham Henry Roberts autobiography, copy of manuscript at Utah State Historical Society, pp. 117-78.

[29]*Salt Lake Tribune,* 6 April 1895.

[30]*Salt Lake Tribune,* 4 April 1895.

[31]*Deseret News,* 5 April 1895.

[32]Franklin D. Richards Journal, 4 April 1895; *Salt Lake Tribune; Deseret News,* 6 April 1895.

[33]*Deseret News,* 10 April 1895.

[34]A. H. Cannon Journal, 11, 12 April 1895; also see Franklin D. Richards Journal, 11 April 1895.

[35]A. H. Cannon Journal, 12 April 1895.

[36]Franklin D. Richards Journal, 18 April 1895; Wells Diaries, 18 April 1895.

[37]John T. Caine to Hamilton Willcox, 11 May 1895, Caine Letterbooks, 1891-95, Church Archives.

[38]*Deseret News,* 13 May 1895. For details of this visit, see Anthony's Diary for 1895; Anna Howard Shaw, *The Story of a Pioneer* (New York: Harper, 1915); Franklin D. Richards Journal, 25 April; 12 May 1895; Wells Diaries, 12-15 May 1895.

[39]Shaw, p. 283.

[40]A. H. Cannon Journal, 21 July 1895.

[41]A. H. Cannon Journal, 30 July 1895.

[42]A. H. Cannon Journal, 8 August 1895.

[43]For an account of Anderson's Court case and the impact upon subsequent elections, see Jean Bickmore White, "Gentle Persuaders, Utah's First Women Legislators," *Utah Historical Quarterly* 38 (Winter 1970): 31-49.

[44]A. H. Cannon Journal, 8 September 1895.

[45]White, "Gentle Persuaders," p. 21.

VI. EQUAL SUFFRAGE IN COLORADO

From nature, education and principle I am a Democrat, consequently, opposed to negro suffrage in any shape or form. Are the supporters of this measure aware that in passing this bill as it now reads, they confer upon negro wenches the right to vote?

M.S. Taylor speaking before the
Colorado Territorial Legislature
January 19, 1870

Warning the representatives in the Colorado territorial house that black women, as well as Chinese women, would be allowed to vote if the election bill which included a clause allowing woman suffrage was passed, Representative M. S. Taylor urged his colleagues not to erect a "monument of their folly" by voting for this piece of legislation.[1] Taylor argued for the maintenance of the electoral system established in 1861 with the creation of the territory of Colorado in which every male person of the age of twenty-one and upwards, not being a Negro or mulatto, and having resided in the territory for six months, was a qualified voter. The Fourteenth Amendment had made the exclusion of black men illegal; nonetheless, Taylor was not willing to admit women to the political arena, especially not black or oriental women.

Representative Taylor was not the first person to discuss the enfranchisement of women in Colorado. The question of woman suffrage had first been raised in Colorado in 1868 when the Eastern press and national congressmen had suggested that the idea be tested in the territories. Noting that traditional treatment of women was an injustice second only to the treatment of blacks, Representative David M. Richards had urged the 1868 Colorado territorial legislature to consider granting women the vote. Though his effort was supported by the former governor, John Evans, Richards' proposal was generally ignored by the lawmakers.[2]

The territorial newspapers, led by Denver's *Rocky Mountain News*, stimulated a lively debate in which the usual arguments on both sides of the question were aired. The opponents warned: Women do not want to vote; only the class which goes to war should be allowed to vote; the enfranchisement of women at this time is premature; and if women are permitted to vote, then black and oriental women will also have access to the voting booth. On the other side, the advocates argued that it was unjust to prohibit women from voting; in some cases, it amounted to taxation without representation.

When the popular St. Louis suffragist Redelia Bates, who was on a lecture tour of the West in 1869, stopped in Denver to speak, she encountered an audience which had already had considerable exposure to the subject of woman suffrage. Yet she found her plea for universal suffrage was not endorsed by a large segment of the population.

Women's rights had been a subject of popular discussion in Colorado for two years when Governor Edward M. McCook, in his first address before the territorial legislature in 1870, recommended that Colorado join its sister territory, Wyoming, as a leader in the cause of universal suffrage. Immediately some legislators took a stand against woman suffrage simply because the governor endorsed it. Many Democratic lawmakers opposed McCook and everything he stood for simply because he had been appointed by President Grant. To them McCook was an outsider and a Republican.

Nevertheless, an election bill which dealt with woman suffrage was studied by a special committee chaired by Representative A. H. DeFrance. Ultimately the committee reported the bill favorably with DeFrance arguing that it was unfair for uneducated, nonproperty-holding black men to vote on matters concerning the property of white women who were not allowed to vote; moreover, he suggested that women's presence in politics would have a purifying influence on society and politics. It was in response to DeFrance's arguments in support of the measure that Representative Taylor delivered his aggressive speech warning the representatives of the folly of allowing black and Chinese women to vote. Undecided, the lower house members referred the measure back to the special committee and invited outsiders to provide them with more information. Consequently, prominent Denver attorney Willard Teller spoke to them in support of woman suffrage, while George A. Hinsdale, president of the legislative council, presented an opposing opinion.

The *Rocky Mountain News* reported that women were urged to air their views to the legislators. Although petitions from women requesting suffrage were presented, there is no evidence that any women took advantage of this invitation to appear before the lawmakers. Thus credence was given to the argument that women really did not want to vote. Finally, DeFrance sought a compromise by recommending that the suffrage bill be amended to provide for its submission to the qualified electors of the territory, including women, for ratification or rejection. After this amendment was accepted, the remainder of the legislative day of February 10, 1870, was spent in parliamentary maneuvering by the friends and foes of women suffrage, ending with the house resolving itself into the committee of the whole and Representative Taylor moving to postpone the bill indefinitely. The motion for postponement passed by a vote of fifteen to ten.

Governor McCook's suggestion was given similar consideration in the territorial council. Here, also, Hinsdale, president of the council, took the opportunity to warn that it was not likely that women would purify politics. On the contrary, there was a possibility, as he phrased it, that politics might destroy "the symmetry of women's character." In spite of Hinsdale's presentation, two days before the house's postponement vote which effectively killed legislation possibilities, the council had passed the woman suffrage measure by one vote.[3]

Even though the legislative measure was dead, the debate continued in the newspapers, and the discussion was periodically enlivened by the visit to the territory of a suffrage lecturer such as Olive Logan, who spoke in Denver on women's rights in July of 1870. One year later Susan B. Anthony and Elizabeth Cady Stanton made a brief stopover in Denver where they were the guests of Governor and Mrs. McCook. Following an enthusiastic welcome, the two suffragists lectured to a large, responsive audience at the Denver Theatre. The press generally praised Anthony's address, but a writer in the *Rocky Mountain News* objected to Stanton's speech, thus drawing her wrath. On Sunday before departing for Laramie, Stanton took the *News* to task for the disrespectful manner in which it sometimes treated the subject of women voting.

After Stanton and Anthony left the territory, the debate on woman suffrage languished. Nevertheless, a few women went to the polls and voted in areas where there were sympathetic registrars. On one occasion a candidate for the position of postmaster in Greeley went so far as to make it part of his campaign to beseech women to go the the polls and vote for him.

When a constitutional committee was preparing the document which would be presented for Colorado's admittance as the Centennial State, the subject of woman suffrage was again discussed throughout the territory. Newspaper support for a woman suffrage clause was generally abundant, especially in Denver. Pueblo's *Colorado Chieftain,* however, insisted Colorado did not need what it referred to as a "Wyoming harvest," and the editor ridiculed suffragists as being "faded and awfully frigid." The other principal spokesman against the concept of universal suffrage was Denver's Catholic Reverend Joseph P. Machebeuf.

While the constitutional convention was in session, a woman suffrage convention was held in Denver. Margaret W. Campbell of Massachusetts, who had been touring northern Colorado for two months delivering addresses, had urged the proponents of woman suffrage to organize their efforts in order to secure a place in the new constitution. An association was formed with Dr. Alida C. Avery as its president, and a suffrage lecture was delivered by long-time supporter David M. Richards. In addition, messages were read from Lucy Stone of Boston and Governor Thayer and Judge Kingman of Wyoming. At its annual convention, the National Woman Suffrage Association resolved that if Colorado would come into the union in a manner befitting for the celebration for the centennial of the Declaration of Independence, she should give the ballot to brothers and sisters, husbands and wives, and thus present to the nation a truly free state.

Despite the fact that Eastern suffrage associations and Colorado women, led by Dr. Avery, presented petitions requesting the ballot for Colorado women, the committee members on suffrage and elections expressed the fear that the whole constitution would be rejected by the Colorado electorate or by the national Congress if woman suffrage was included. Thus they limited the electorate to adult males. They allowed, however, that there would be no distinction on account of sex in school district elections.

As a result of the efforts of the prosuffrage delegates, Henry P. H. Bromwell and Agipeta Vigil, who were the only two members of the committee on suffrage who did not support the manhood suffrage report, an additional statement was included in the explanatory article of the new constitution which specified that suffrage requirements could be changed at any time. Moreover, there was an order instructing the general assembly to submit the question of woman suffrage to a direct vote of the people at the first general election after the achievement of statehood which, if the constitution was accepted, would be the autumn of 1877. Finally, the male suffrage constitution was adopted and Colorado was admitted to the union.

Even after statehood was realized, legislators Bromwell and Vigil continued to push for woman suffrage. Henry P. H. Bromwell had a long record of sympathy for women's rights. Prior to moving to Colorado he had been the Republican congressman from Illinois and reportedly had spoken out in favor of women when the Illinois constitution had been under consideration. Vigil, on the other hand, was a Spanish-speaking stockman, originally from Taos, who represented the constituency of southern Colorado. As Vigil reported the story he had been converted to the cause of woman suffrage by Mary F. Shields of Colorado Springs.

Immediately after Colorado entered the union as the Centennial State, legislators, led by Bromwell and Vigil, submitted the question of woman suffrage to the electorate. The referendum was to be decided at the general election on October 2, 1877. With ten months before the decision was to be made, the Colorado Suffrage Association launched its campaign. Among the members of the seventeen-person committee appointed to district the state and send out speakers for women suffrage was William H. Bright, who had initiated the woman suffrage bill in Wyoming and was now living in Denver.

Again newspaper space was available for advocates on both sides of the question. The most vigorous words against the idea were still seen on the pages of the *Colorado Chieftain*. Likewise, Reverend Machebeuf continued his pulpit campaigning against women's rights. Before long he was joined by the Presbyterian, Reverend Mr. Bliss, who referred to suffragists as "bawling, ranting women, bristling for their rights" and warned his parishioners that if women were allowed to vote then married women would live in endless bickering with their husbands while single women would never marry. In other words, the tradition of home and family would be endangered.[4]

With the election less than a month away, September was a lively campaign time. The Colorado Suffrage Association had coordinated a speaking program which had brought many Eastern headliners to the mining towns of Colorado. Susan B. Anthony, who had been lecturing for the Slayton Bureau in the Mid-West, cancelled her tour and joined the campaign in Colorado. She stumped many mining towns and outlying communities in the southern part of the state, urging the men to cast their votes in favor of political rights for women. Speaking in saloons, in hotel dining rooms, at railroad stations, or from a soap box in front of a courthouse, she sought support for the referendum. Frequently, she was frustrated because the men in the audience did not seem to know what she wanted them to do. Sometimes, she felt, the men had had so much liquor they could not follow her arguments. On other occasions it was simply because the Spanish-speaking miners did not understand English. Anthony was discouraged, but she persisted. At Oro City the prosuffragist governor, John L. Routt, stood by her side as she lectured to a saloon crowd, and he closed the meeting by adding his endorsement to her requests.

In addition to Anthony, other visiting lecturers toured Colorado. Escorted by her husband, Mary W. Campbell traveled about the state by carriage, delivering the message of women's rights. Meanwhile, Matilda Hindman of Pennsylvania, acclaimed as the most effective campaigner, visited towns which could be reached by rail. A lesser known spokeswoman from Philadelphia, Lelia Partridge, also toured the state. Both the National and American woman suffrage associations threw their support behind the effort in Colorado. Lucy Stone and Henry Blackwell journeyed from Boston to aid in the campaign. Since there was such an all out effort in Colorado, the American Woman Suffrage Association even cancelled its annual convention in 1877 to focus on the Colorado campaign.[5]

Western advocates of woman suffrage were also active in the campaign. Judge John W. Kingman was invited down from Wyoming to testify about the experience there. Wyoming's other pioneer advocate of woman suffrage, William H. Bright, was interviewed on the subject of woman suffrage in the territory of Wyoming. Campaign speakers also included veteran Colorado suffragists such as former governor Evans, legislator Henry Bromwell, and lawyer David M. Richards. In addition, Mary F. Shields used her "motherly approach" to convince citizens of northern Colorado that they should support the idea of women being allowed at the polls.

The day before the election the suffragists held their final rally in Denver, and on election day they appeared at the polling places to hand out literature and try to persuade the men to vote in the affirmative. In Denver, Lucy Stone was distributing suffrage fliers to the men approaching the voting booths, but when she attempted to provide Reverend Bliss with a handout, he immediately identified himself and reiterated his objections to women voting. Lucy Stone countered and a loud exchange ensued. Yet when the day was ended Reverend Bliss' point of view was victorious.

When the votes were tallied the measure was defeated by a vote of two to one out of a total of nearly thirty thousand voters. The centers of support for woman suffrage proved to be in Denver where most of the vocal suffragists lived and in Greeley where "five out of seven of her voters declared for women suffrage."[6] The women lecturers had not been able to convince the voters from the small towns. Generally, the mining districts and southern counties returned large negative votes.[7] Later Anthony would show her animosity against the Spanish-speaking citizens by blaming them for the defeat of the measure in the southern counties. The evidence, however, indicates that a large number of Anglo males also voted against the woman suffrage proposal.

108

Lucy Stone

Jubilant about the defeat of what they referred to as "windy fanatics" who had tried to force woman suffrage on the people of Colorado, the *Colorado Chieftain* editors bid adieu to the Eastern suffragists chastizing them for interfering in Colorado's affairs. Once the Easterners had gone, the discouraged local suffragists allowed the suffrage dialogue to subside. Even the "Woman's Column" in the *Rocky Mountain News* was discontinued. For the next sixteen years there was no concentrated effort on behalf of woman suffrage in Colorado.

There were random petitions to the state legislature requesting political rights for women and some efforts were made by suffragists to educate the public, but during the 1880s little progress towards equal suffrage was realized in Colorado. Even Dr. Avery and Mary Shields, who had been actively involved with the National Suffrage Association from 1876 through 1879, no longer served as officers or attended the national meetings.[8] The state's suffragists formed themselves into an Equal Rights League, but it soon died. In 1881 another effort was made to form a Colorado Equal Suffrage Association, and the suffrage newspaper *Queen Bee* was launched. But the Colorado legislature's refusal to pass legislation granting women municipal suffrage was more symbolic of the events that year.

In spite of the lack of enthusiasm for woman suffrage, Mrs. C. M. Churchill urged women to make their influence felt even if it was not wanted and to show that they were a political force. Mrs. Churchill's *Queen Bee*, as its masthead declared, was a newspaper advocating "Women's Political Equality and Individuality." Churchill's crusade for woman suffrage went to the extent of urging women to go to the polls and vote even though it was illegal. In addition, the columns of the *Bee* were used to speak out against liquor, against dance halls, against tobacco, against divorce, against Catholics, and against Mormons. However, there was not much happening in Colorado concerning woman suffrage in the decade following statehood.

In 1890, while campaigning in South Dakota to have the word "male" removed from that proposed state's admitting constitution, Matilda Hindman again visited Denver on a fund raising tour. While there she persuaded the local friends of woman suffrage to form a state association. In her rooms at the Richelieu Hotel, she oversaw the organization of the Colorado Equal Suffrage Association Education Committee, which was to concentrate its efforts on educating the public on the subject of women's political rights through the use of study sessions. Louise M. Tyler later stimulated this association to establish a constitution and bylaws and to hold regular meetings. Louise Tyler had moved from Boston to Denver in 1890 bringing along an invitation from Lucy Stone to the women of Colorado to join as an auxiliary of the recently merged National American Woman Suffrage Association. When Harriet Scott Saxton ran for a place on the east Denver school board, the newly formed suffrage association endorsed her and supported her fruitless campaign.

Despite petitions from women, the 1891 legislature rejected an amendment to the state constitution which would have allowed women to vote. The 1893 general assembly, however, decided that the question should be submitted to the electorate again at the next general election. As a result of the sympathetic support of Populist legislators and the work of the suffrage association, a bill was passed which provided:

That every female person shall be entitled to vote at all elections in the same manner in all respects as male persons are, or shall be entitled to vote by the constitution and laws of this state, and the same qualification as to age, citizenship and time of residence in the state, county, city, ward and precinct and all other qualifications required by law to entitle male persons to vote shall be required to entitle female persons to vote.[9]

It was Populist party support which made the 1893 effort a success. In the lower house one Democrat voted for the bill and three against; eleven Republicans voted for the bill and twenty-one against; twenty-two Populists voted in favor, three against. In the state senate not one Democrat supported the bill, all five were opposed to it; eight Republicans voted in favor, five against; while twelve Populists voted for and only one against. As soon as the measure was passed, it was signed by the Populist governor, David H. Waite, who earlier had recommended municipal suffrage for women in his message to the legislature. Thus a woman suffrage measure was once again submitted to the male voters of the Centennial State.

With twenty-five dollars in its treasury and twenty-eight members, the Colorado Woman Suffrage Association changed its name to the Non-Partisan Equal Suffrage Association and launched a campaign to persuade a majority of Colorado's men to mark their ballots: "EQUAL SUFFRAGE APPROVED" rather than "EQUAL SUFFRAGE NOT APPROVED."

While Colorado voters were discussing the pros and cons of supporting the referendum to allow women access to the ballot, the means whereby woman suffrage could best be achieved throughout the world were being considered by the Woman's Congress which was meeting in Chicago in conjunction with the 1893 World's Columbian Exposition. Thus the vice president of the Colrado suffrage association, Ellis Meredith Stansbury,[10] attended the Woman's Congress where she appealed to the National American Woman Suffrage Association for assistance in the Colorado campaign. In response the association sent Carrie Lane Chapman Catt to the mile high city to lend her organizing abilities and lecturing experience to the cause. In addition, Laura Ormiston Chant of London appeared and delivered two suffrage addresses in Denver.

Remembering the unsuccessful 1877 referendum experience, the Colorado suffragists prepared for the new fight. Local suffrage leagues were organized throughout the state and mass meetings were held. Unlike the 1877 crusade, however, in this campaign they invited few Eastern women to Colorado to stump the state. Instead, the suffragists concentrated on converting the male voters through the newspapers and through the political parties.

Ellis Meredith Stansbury

In the 1893 Denver school district elections, the women demonstrated that they understood political power. Since women were allowed to vote in school elections, they sponsored Ione T. Hanna for school district director, then turned out in large numbers to elect her. In so doing, they countered the frequently heard argument that women did not want to vote.

Favorable newspaper and political support encouraged the suffrage campaigners. Almost all the Denver newspapers editorialized in favor of equality for women; in fact, three-quarters of all newspapers in the state seemed to support the idea of women voting. The *Denver Republican* provided space for Patience Stapleton to discuss suffrage; while the *Rocky Mountain News* revived the "Woman's Column" for Ellis Meredith Stansbury and Minnie J. Reynolds.

Three political parties—the Republicans, the Prohibitionists, and the People's party—endorsed the concept of equal suffrage. The Populists even had an equal suffrage plank in their 1893 national platform. Having changed their views, the miners and other unionized workers now seemed willing to support the suffrage organization since women were pledging their support to the silver issue. As a demonstration of their support the Knights of Labor sent Leonora Barry Lake of St. Louis to Colorado to help in the suffrage campaign.

The well-organized Colorado Women's Christian Temperance Union also supported the suffrage campaign to the extent of sponsoring their president on a five-month suffrage speaking tour in the state. In spite of the identification of temperance with suffrage, there seemed to be little hostility from the liquor interests. Only one pamphlet ridiculing and abusing supporters of women's rights was circulated. On the whole, the traditional opponents seemed generally uninterested in the contest. It was not until the eve of the election that the brewers distributed fliers warning against enfranchising women.

As a consequence of strong support and little opposition, the referendum succeeded. The returns showed that 35,698 voters supported the statute to allow woman suffrage, while 29,461 opposed it. Generally, Populist counties approved the change, while the Republican and Democratic controlled areas did not. The state legislature in its resolution submitting the question to the voters had provided that if the referendum were successful it would become effective as soon as a proclamation was made by the governor. Eighteen days after election day the women of Colorado staged a demonstration commemorating the equal suffrage victory, and Populist Governor Waite presented a proclamation giving the women of the state equal franchise with the men. In so doing, he increased the voting population of the state by about forty percent.

Immediately the suffrage women organized study clubs to examine parliamentary rules and make themselves familiar with the political economy of the day. John Fisk's *Civil Government in the United States* was in great demand by the women who wanted to prepare themselves to intelligently exercise their newly gained political rights. In the 1894 Colorado elections, women voted for the first time. No unpleasant results were apparent as the consequence of the voting by women according to Senator Wolcott and Senator Henry M. Teller, the brother of Willard Teller who in 1870 had spoke in favor of woman suffrage before the territorial legislature. The two senators summarized women's role in Colorado politics for Senator Hoar of Massachusetts, assuring him "that the undefined fear that the bestowal of the right might lead to certain offensive demonstrations of what is termed the strongmindedness of women had found no justification."[11]

Once they had achieved their goal, many Colorado women went to work to help others realize political power. In 1895, when Utah citizens were debating whether or not to accept the proposed state constitution which included a woman suffrage clause, a delegation of suffragists form Colorado—Mary Carroll Craig Bradford and Ellis Meredith Stansbury—accompanied Susan B. Anthony and Anna Howard Shaw to Utah where they held a suffrage conference. The following year the Colorado Equal Suffrage Association raised funds and sent Mary C. C. Bradford to Idaho to assist in the effort to amend that state's constitution to allow for woman suffrage.

While the question of woman suffrage had been under consideration in Colorado in 1893, the Wyoming state legislature had passed a resolution urging all areas of the world to enfranchise their female residents. After five years of experience with equal suffrage, the Colorado General Assembly followed Wyoming's example by declaring woman suffrage a success and recommending that every state and territory of the American union enfranchise their women.

As time passed Coloradans became more and more confident of the rightness of their decision. During the 1896 campaign in California, Ida A. Harper, in an article in the *San Francisco Call,* quoted Colorado Governor McIntyre as saying woman suffrage was a decided success and that women were voting in as large a proportion as the men. After the women of the state had been legally voting for nine years, the Colorado constitution was officially amended changing the wording specifying electors from "all males" to "every person."

Without a doubt it was Populist support that had meant success for women suffrage in Colorado. Generally, Populists supported women's rights. In return, some women supported the Populists. In 1894 suffragist and lawyer, Phoebe Couzins, came to Colorado to aid the Populists in their campaign. The women of Colorado, like the men, supported William Jennings Bryan in the 1896 election.

Wyoming was the first state to grant its women the ballot, but suffragists quickly seized Colorado as a more attractive example because the latter state had a larger population and a large urban center where the impact of women voting could be closely observed. Moreover, Wyoming's reputation as a wide-open frontier community with a high crime level made it a poor example, and Utah was a totally unacceptable example because it was tainted by polygamy.

In addition, Colorado was unique in that it was the first state to grant woman suffrage by a popular referendum. The methods used by the suffragists in Colorado would serve as a model for workers in other state referendum campaigns. Unlike Wyoming and Utah where the territorial legislature and governor or a constitutional convention had acted on their own, in Colorado women had waged an aggressive campaign for the ballot in which they had received financial and organizational support from the Eastern suffrage organizations. The strategy of converting the male electorate through suffragists' speeches, party organizations, and public demonstrations, which was perfected in Colorado under the guidance of Carrie Chapman Catt, would be employed in other areas, notably California and Idaho.

Notes

[1]"Speech of M. S. Taylor on Suffrage," *Colorado Transcript*, 26 January 1870.

[2]For details of events related to woman suffrage in Colorado, I am indebted to the comprehensive study done by Billie Barnes Jensen for her masters thesis at the University of Colorado in 1959; since that time she has published her findings in articles in the *Colorado Magazine* and *The Journal of the West*. Another earlier detailed history of equal suffrage in Colorado was published by Joseph G. Brown in 1898. In 1956 William B. Faherty presented a study in the *Colorado Magazine* in which he examined the relationship between woman suffrage and regional minorities which pointed to some of the racist overtones of the debate in Colorado. *The History of Woman Suffrage* contains two chapters on Colorado, 3:712-25; 4:509-34.

[3]Jensen, M. A. thesis, pp. 20-21.

[4]*History of Woman Suffrage*, 3:723.

[5]National American Woman Suffrage Association File, Library of Congress Manuscript Division.

[6]Brown, p. 14.

[7]Jensen, M. A. thesis, p. 55a and Appendix B.

[8]Elizabeth Cady Stanton Papers, Carton 7, Library of Congress Manuscript Division. Avery was cited as vice president from Colorado and Shields was noted as a member of the national advisory committee in 1876 and 1879; a list of officers is included in Tract No. 1 of the National Woman Suffrage Association, Boston Public Library, Boston, Mass.

[9]Brown, p. 24.

[10]Ellis Meredith Stansbury was the daughter of suffragist Emily Meredith. In the nineteenth century press, Ellis is referred to as Lyle Meredith Stansbury and Mrs. H. S. Stansbury. For clarity she is consistently referred to as Ellis Meredith Stansbury in this study.

[11]*Deseret News*, 21 February 1895.

VII. THE SUFFRAGE IDEA IN IDAHO

Grant us the right of suffrage. . .and. . .we will proclaim the glad tidings of our freedom among all the crowded states and cities of the East, and in so doing. . .turn the tide of immigration to Idaho.

Abigail Scott Duniway
Path Breaking

The often heard claim that woman suffrage would bring a flood of settlers into a region was largely discredited after Wyoming's initial experience, but some advocates of woman suffrage such as Abigail Scott Duniway, editor of the suffrage newsletter *The New Northwest*, persisted in using it. Oregon suffragist Duniway advised Idaho legislators that "the tide of immigration" could be turned into Idaho if women there were enfranchised. Yet, within Idaho, the population was not an important factor in the woman suffrage debate. Of far greater importance were the examples of women voting in the surrounding regions. If women were enfranchised in Wyoming and Utah, why should they not enjoy the same right in Idaho?[1]

A year after women were granted the vote in the two neighboring territories of Wyoming and Utah, a similar piece of legislation was presented to the Idaho legislators. In the sixth session of the Idaho territorial legislature, a woman suffrage bill was introduced in the lower house by the Democratic representative from Oneida county, Dr. Joseph William Morgan. Once Morgan had let it be known that he proposed amending the election law to extend the franchise to women, his fellow lawmakers designated him chairman of all activities relating to women. Consequently, he was "made the committee of reception" in charge of food and drink for ladies day at the legislature. Within a week after this reception, many of the women were back on the floor of the assembly to witness the final phase of the debate on the woman suffrage issue.

Reportedly, Dr. Morgan held up his end of the ensuing debate with sincerity and "much skill." He argued for the enfranchisement of women on the premise of the consent of the governed. Voices were also heard on the other side of the question. The most forceful spokesman against the measure was Republican W. H. Van Slyke who began his rebuttal with the Blackstonian stand that the family was one and the woman merged with the man upon marriage and henceforth was represented by the man. Then he went on to warn: "That to give her the ballot would work an entire social revolution, disrupting the family tie, and bringing a conflict of sexes in the land."[2] Apparently, Van Slyke's Blackstonian appeal and Morgan's liberal tradition arguments were both persuasive. When the lawmakers put the issue to a vote, it resulted in a tie. Thus, Idaho's first woman suffrage bill died.

In order to understand the motivation behind this early effort to enfranchise the female citizens of Idaho, one must know something about Joseph Morgan.

116

Joseph William Morgan

Dr. Morgan may have been a Mormon. The Welsh physician had immigrated with his family from Great Britain to Salt Lake City, then to the Mormon community of Malad. Even if he was not a member of the church, a large percentage of his constituency certainly was. In this period approximately one fourth of Idaho residents were Mormon. In 1871 most of the Mormon settlements along the border between Idaho and Utah were part of Oneida county, which at that time, comprised the present-day counties of Bear Lake, Bannock, Bingham, Caribou, Fremont, and Oneida. Just the year before the dividing line between the two territories had been made clear with the consequence that many residents of these Mormon settlements discovered that they were officially part of Idaho Territory instead of Utah Territory as they had thought. The first year many of the residents of these communities were assessed taxes in Idaho was 1870.[3] Thus it can be concluded that most Mormons in the southern settlements whom Dr. Morgan represented were aware of the operation of woman suffrage in Utah Territory; some of the women may have even voted in 1870 when they thought their communities were part of Utah Territory.

Certainly this early drive to enfranchise women in Idaho was influenced by events in the neighboring territories of Wyoming and Utah and by discussions of the subject on the national scene. Suffrage lecturers, however, were not as important in Idaho as elsewhere. Since the transcontinental railroad did not cross Idaho, the Eastern suffragists and lecturers who visited Wyoming, Colorado, and Utah could not easily carry their messages to Idaho. As reported in the *Idaho Statesman*, the first woman to ascend a platform and deliver a lecture in Boise was an Idaho lawyer by the name of Young, who spoke on women suffrage in 1872. Usually cited as "Mrs. Young" and sometimes as "Carrie F. Young," this might have been one individual or two, one of which might have been Helen L. Young who lived in the northern Idaho communites of Wallace and Osburn and was heralded as Idaho's first woman lawyer. When Young had participated in the Pacific Coast suffrage convention in San Francisco two years earlier, reporters there had described "Mrs. Young of Idaho" as a "little brown mouse" who was "brimful of sunshine and happy thoughts." During Victoria Woodhull's campaign for the Presidency, some Idahoans accused Young of being affiliated with the candidate's free-love crusade simply because they both advocated woman suffrage. However, the editor of the *Idaho Statesman*, a Boise-based newspaper affiliated with the Republican party, came to the defense of this early suffrage and temperance lecturer in Idaho.[4] In so doing, the *Statesman* editor initiated what would prove to be a long liaison with the woman suffrage movement.

With the exception of an occasional speech by "Mrs. Young," there was not much activity in Idaho related to woman suffrage for the decade and a half after the failure of Dr. Morgan's bill. What activity there was centered around the personality of Abigail Scott Duniway of Portland, Oregon, who in 1871 launched her weekly newspaper *The New Northwest* which was devoted to women's rights. Copies of this newspaper were distributed in Idaho; in fact, Duniway frequently visited Idaho to lecture and to solicit subscribers.

Acclaimed as "the best lady talker on this coast," Duniway preached women's rights to Idaho citizens. In so doing, she often attacked the experiment with woman suffrage in Utah, saying Mormon women were mere slaves being used by the male hierarchy to hold ascendency over non-Mormons. On the other hand, she praised woman suffrage in Wyoming and Washington territories, saying these were the only valid experiments.

On one occasion Duniway went so far as to tell Idaho residents that immigrants were going to Washington Territory rather than settling in the "Gem of the mountains" because women were allowed to vote in the more westerly territory. Milton Kelly, founder and editor of the *Statesman* exposed the absurdity of this assertion by declaring: "Nobody has gone to Washington Territory because women are permitted to vote there, and probably nobody has stayed away or declined to emigrate there on that account."[5] Although critical of those who argued that enfranchising women of the territory would prompt people to move to Idaho; he was a strong advocate of woman suffrage. Editor Kelly's wife, who has been called "the pioneer suffragist of Idaho"[6] encouraged this editorial stance. In the 1800's, long before there was a suffrage organization in Idaho, Mrs. Milton Kelly was attending the annual conferences of the National Woman Suffrage Association and encouraging woman suffragists at home.

In spite of the *Stateman's* editorials, in Idaho the woman suffrage issue was intertwined with the immigration and Mormon questions. Like other western territories, Idaho was interested in growth and development; yet there is little evidence that many people believed woman suffrage would have much impact on the flow of settlers one way or the other. There were, however, those who feared that if women were enfranchised it would give the Mormons in the territory disproportionate political power since there were many more women proportionately in the Mormon settlements than in the rest of the territory. Some Idaho citizens were afraid that such a measure might also encourage more Mormons to move to Idaho. Many of these same people felt that "the impression was getting abroad that Idaho was controlled by the leading Mormons in Salt Lake, and that this impression would tend to discourage [non-Mormon] immigration."[7]

The underlying cause of most of this concern was political anxiety. In 1881 Republican John B. Neil, who had spent some time in Salt Lake City prior to the time that President Hayes had appointed him to head the government in Idaho, suggested that all Mormons in Idaho be disfranchised, since reportedly most of the Mormons, who composed about one-fourth of the territory's population, voted Democratic. The largely Democratic legislature ignored the governor's suggestion, but four years later when they prepared to rewrite their election statute the lawmakers considered disfranchising Mormons and enfranchising women.

Nonetheless, the woman suffrage question was not a partisan issue in Idaho. There were supporters and opponents of women's right to vote in both parties. The Idaho Republican party came out in favor of woman suffrage, but obviously many Republicans were concerned about the balance of political power if the large

Mrs. Milton Kelly

number of Mormon women in the territory were admitted to the polls. Finally, they compromised by allowing women to vote in elections for county school superintendents. The editor of the *Boise City Republican* justified such an extension of the franchise as follows:

> Women being naturally gifted as teachers, we see no reason why they should not be competent to judge the qualifications necessary for teaching, which is the only matter which the law intrusts [*sic.*] to the sole judgement of the Superintendent.[8]

The following year Mormons were barred from teaching in Idaho's public schools. Then a delegation of Idahoans took the larger question of Mormon rights to the national Congress; they requested that all men and women connected with polygamy or Mormonism, regardless of the territory of their residence, be barred from voting, holding office, or locating on public lands.[9] Mormons' access to the ballot and women's right to vote were discussed whenever Idaho considered the definition of the electorate. By the mid 1880s Idaho had an election law which required a test oath for membership in an organization which advocated polygamy. Thus all members of the Mormon church, regardless of whether they believed in or practiced plural marriage, could be denied access to the polling booth. Once the Mormon question was settled in this law, which for all practical purposes disfranchised all Mormons in Idaho, the woman suffrage question could be considered independent of polygamy.

In 1887 Abigail Duniway addressed the Idaho territorial legislature on woman suffrage. Since she had abandoned her journalistic endeavor and had moved from Oregon to Custer county, Idaho, where her sons had filed a homestead claim, she could now speak to the lawmakers as an Idaho resident. The truth of the matter, however, was that she spent most of her time going back and forth from Idaho to the Northwest pursuing suffrage activities. As a result of her appeal, the Idaho legislators briefly considered a female enfranchisement bill but ultimately abandoned it.[10]

Railroad construction in Idaho in the 1880s made the area more accessible; the Oregon Short Line from Wyoming to Oregon via Boise made east-west travel across the territory possible, and the Mormon rail from Utah through the Snake River Valley to Butte, Montana, connected the Union Pacific and Northern Pacific. With the improved transportation in Idaho, an Eastern suffragist ventured into the area. Clara B. Colby, editor of the National Woman Suffrage Association's newspaper, the *Woman's Tribune,* while on a lecture tour of the Pacific Northwest and Utah, visited Mountain Home, Idaho. Her brief suffrage speech there sparked a lively newspaper debate. A Mountain Home resident by the name of Homer Stull could not resist the temptation to counter Colby's assumptions with the following arguments: "The Creator has planted men and women in families," and in order that this arrangement shall persist it is necessary for one person to leave the home to earn the means to maintain it while the other person must remain at home

121

Abigail Scott Duniway

"to care for its domestic life and give almost uninterrupted attention to the welfare of the children." Stull felt this "natural division of labor" would be threatened if women were allowed to vote; for as he said, "if women are to vote they must hold office an assume and equal position with men in all public affairs."[11] Local feminist Jennie Bearby defended Clara Colby and woman suffrage by reminding Mr. Stull that the whole world did not fit into his idealized system. As she said, "man and woman are one; but the man is the one, and in many homes where there is no man there is no representation." She went on to cite Wyoming and Washington as regions where woman suffrage existed without an "irreparable injury to homes."[12]

The facts were, however, that the franchise granted to the women of Washington Territory in 1883 had been declared unconstitutional. One of the reasons Clara Colby and her suffrage colleague Elizabeth Saxon had been in the Northwest was to attempt to forestall such action. Nevertheless, the justices of the territorial supreme court had ruled that the woman suffrage bill was not in conformity with the territory organic act which they determined used the term "citizen" only to mean male citizens; therefore the legislature had authority only to endow male citizens with the franchise. Consequently, female citizens were declared ineligible to act as electors or jurors. The Washington territorial legislature would later pass another suffrage bill, but the territorial supreme court would again overturn the law.

Many suffragists, including Abigail Duniway, blamed the Women's Christian Temperance Union's efforts to stop liquor traffic for the reversal of Washington's suffrage law. Agitation by temperance workers reportedly created anxiety among the liquor interests that the women would use the ballot to achieve prohibition. Thus Duniway cautioned Idaho suffragists not to allow themselves to be identified with prohibition.

It is understandable, therefore, that Duniway was concerned when she heard that the constitutional convention, meeting in Boise in 1889 to draw up a document whereby Idaho could join the union, was being petitioned by the Idaho Women's Christian Temperance Union for the inclusion in the constitution of a clause prohibiting the sale of liquor and one enfranchising women. Immediately she rushed to appear before the convention. She wanted to convince the delegates that temperance and woman suffrage were not inexorably tied, and she wanted to assure them that women would not necessarily vote away beer and whiskey. Her efforts were to no avail, neither item was included in the constitution. Duniway went away convinced that the fear of a temperance crusade which she felt had been stimulated by the activities of the Women's Christian Temperance Union had kept the delegates from including a woman suffrage clause in the constitution. But the fact of the matter was that the convention delegates seemed to be more afraid that the constitution would not be accepted if they included woman suffrage than they were that women would use the vote to bring about prohibition.

After the convention Duniway noted her disappointment but reported that she had been able to extract a pledge from the leaders of the convention assuring her that an equal suffrage amendment would be submitted to the electorate by an act of the first state legislature. She had not been able to persuade the delegates to make their pledge part of the constitution as had been done in Colorado however. Thus Idaho voters approved a constitution which allowed for the limitation of the ballot to adult, non-Mormon men. Moreover, neither women nor Mormon men were permitted to vote on the constitution which excluded them from participation in Idaho's political arena.

In 1890 when the United States House of Representatives Committee on Territories was reviewing the constitutions submitted by Idaho and Wyoming in their bids for admittance into the union, the Democratic minority spokesman, Representative William M. Springer of Illinois, reported the Democrats' opposition to the Wyoming constitution because it included a clause enfranchising women. They also voted in a bloc against the admission of Idaho because as Springer summarized it: "The Mormons had been disenfranchised in Idaho because it was suspected that they voted the Democratic ticket—but in Wyoming they were permitted to enjoy the rights of citizens because they voted with the Republicans."[13] Nevertheless, both Idaho and Wyoming finally were admitted with the constitutions they had submitted, the first with non-Mormon manhood suffrage, the second with universal suffrage.

Once Idaho became a state there was some activity on the part of women to secure the vote. Mormon women, temperance workers, and Abigail Duniway all worked in their own ways for woman suffrage. In 1892 Utah suffrage campaigners Emmeline B. Wells and Emily S. Richards spread the message of equal suffrage to women in Idaho's Mormon settlements.[14]

The Idaho Women's Christian Temperance Union, led by Henrietta Skelton, continued its suffrage work. The union's franchise department was not strong, but some women's feelings did "run high" on the subject of woman suffrage. When a Boise minister, addressing the 1891 annual convention of the Idaho Union, said he did not know what his duties were since he was only an honorary member of the organization, a woman in the audience instantly replied: "Your position in the union is the same as ours in politics. You pay your money, but you can't vote."[15]

Under the heading "Franchise" the same Women's Christian Temperance convention issued the following proclamation: "Together in the church, at home and at the ballot box, and the knell of the liquor traffic will soon be rung."[16] Statements like this only served to further convince Duniway and others that the Women's Christian Temperance Union's major concern with the ballot in Idaho, as elsewhere, was simply to secure a means whereby prohibition could be achieved. Consequently, what suffrage efforts there were in Idaho were split as the Union campaign was countered by Duniway who feared the liquor interests would be inspired to actively oppose equal suffrage.

When Duniway appeared before the Idaho constitutional convention, she had identified herself as a representative of the National Woman Suffrage Association; nevertheless, she was also in conflict with this organization in that she objected to the association of leading suffragists, including Susan B. Anthony, with the Temperance Union. Moreover, she opposed "hurrah" campaigns, as she called them, and noisy rallies staged by "self-imported suffragists" whenever there was a suffrage campaign in the West. Arguing that the passage of woman suffrage legislation depended on the votes of men, Duniway insisted that the best method was to quietly persuade legislators and male voters of the moral and legal rightness of woman suffrage. She might have questioned her own persuasive powers; however, for the pledge that an equal suffrage amendment would be submitted to the electorate by the first state legislature was not kept.

Even a Republican-sponsored woman suffrage amendment could not get the required two-thirds majority vote in both houses of the legislature in 1893 in order to be sent to the voters for their decision. It was after this defeat that the first woman suffrage organization was formed in Idaho. The school teacher in the small town of Hagerman, Elizabeth Ingram, called some friends together one spring day and launched an independent suffrage society. Unlike the developments in other territories, this organization did not grow and form other chapters. Most discussions of woman suffrage in Idaho remained in the political arena.

The following year the Idaho Populist party, in keeping with the national party platform plank in favor of woman suffrage, announced its support for the amendment of the three-year-old state constitution. The president of the National League of Republican Women, Jane Ellen Foster, who was touring the Western states the summer of 1894, reported from Boise that the Idaho Republican state convention favored woman suffrage, and she went on to predict that an amendment would be on the ballot in the 1896 general election.[17]

Confident that a woman suffrage amendment would be considered at the next election in Idaho, Abigail Duniway attended the 1895 National American Woman Suffrage Association convention in Atlanta, Georgia. At that meeting she presented the report on suffrage work in Oregon. Then, since there was not a suffrage organization in Idaho and there was no official representative from that state, Duniway discussed the upcoming campaign there. In so doing, she made it clear that Eastern suffragists should stay at home unless summoned. She did invite them, however, to assist in the Idaho campaign by sending money.

Upon her return to Idaho, Duniway and the Republican editor of the *Statesman*, William Balderston, launched a suffrage organization for Idaho. Without a doubt, Duniway was an important figure in the early development of the suffrage story in Idaho, but the evidence indicates that events were more complicated and involved more people than she suggested in her "pathbreaking" narrative. For example, when Idahoans recalled this event they reported that "a temporary organization was formed at that time, but for sufficient reasons nothing was done to start the work until some months later."[18] The "sufficient reasons" for delay may have been Duniway's conflict with Idaho and national suffragists. In response to Duniway's declaration that Idaho was off limits to eastern suffragists, Susan B. Anthony, who was on a tour of the West with Anna Howard Shaw, told Duniway to leave suffrage work in Idaho to "Eastern managers" and to confine herself to suffrage activities in Oregon where she now lived.[19] As a result of this decision, Carrie Chapman Catt, organizer for the National American Woman Suffrage Association, sent Emma Smith DeVoe of Illinois to Idaho to manage the campaign. Mell Woods, an active suffrage worker from Wallace, Idaho, who was the daughter of the Mormon woman suffragist Emmeline B. Wells of Salt Lake City, was assigned to assist the national organizer. Once in Idaho, DeVoe launched a lecture tour which took her to the outlying settlements of the state where she organized suffrage clubs as she traveled. In November delegates from such clubs in eight counties converged on Boise where they formed the Idaho Equal Suffrage Association as an auxiliary of the National American Woman Suffrage Association.

Abigail Duniway was not present at the first meeting of this Idaho state suffrage organization, possibly because of her husband's ill health. But this absence, together with the fact that she is not mentioned in the association's minutes, leads to the suspicion that perhaps she exaggerated the importance of her own role in Idaho suffrage affairs. Her outspoken antipathy for Mormonism and Mormon women may have made it impossible for her to work with Mormon women in Idaho such as Mell Woods. This, along with Duniway's conflict with temperance workers and her insistence that Eastern suffragists not meddle in Idaho suffrage activities, may have been one of the reasons why Susan B. Anthony was so emphatic when she told Duniway to stay out of Idaho affairs.

Newspaperman William Balderston, however, was present at the first suffrage association meeting, and he addressed the Idaho suffragists on strategy for securing passage of the woman suffrage amendment to be submitted to the electorate the fall of 1896. In so doing, he endorsed the idea that there should be one representative from each county, but he suggested that the women organize right down to the precinct level. In his closing remarks he expressed the hope that this organizational meeting would show that Idaho women "who are not afraid to lead in the cause are prepared for an aggressive campaign." He attempted to inspire suffragists with his final statement: "Multitudes, both men and women, who are now wavering and uncertain will follow aggressive leadership, and victory will certainly be the reward next fall."[20]

While still in convention the newly organized equal suffrage workers received a telegram from Susan B. Anthony who had just returned to her Buffalo, New York, home from her trip to California where she had worked in that state's unsuccessful suffrage campaign. She advised the Idaho suffragists to "educate rank and file of voters through political party papers and meetings," if they wanted the woman suffrage amendment to carry. Probably recalling her unsuccessful attempt to appeal to miners in the 1877 Colorado referendum effort and her more recent experiences in California, Anthony cautioned that "woman speakers cannot reach them [male voters]."[21]

Declaring their belief that "the ballot is a badge of equality in all classes," the Idaho delegates adjourned their conference with the pledge:

to work in all womanly ways for the advancement of the principles of equality in our state and to secure the adoption of an amendment to our constitution to secure equal civil and political rights for both men and women.[22]

By the spring of 1896 the fledgling suffrage association was organized for the upcoming campaign. National organizer Laura M. Johns, who had come from Salina, Kansas, to assist the Idaho operation, would be responsible for the southwest part of the state and would have her headquarters in Boise. Blanche Whitman of Montpelier would rally the predominantly Mormon communities in the southeast, while Wallace lawyer Helen Young would take charge of the northern part of the state.

In the process of drawing up resolutions asking for passage of the equal suffrage amendment, Idaho suffrage workers pointed to the examples in the neighboring states of Wyoming, Colorado, and Utah, noting that the result of these experiments with women voting had been "altogether good and nothing evil." They also reminded men that the enfranchisement of women was in accord with "the basic principles of our republic" such as the concept of no taxation without representation. Racist appeals were often heard. Suffragists argued that white, native-born American women should be at least equal in political rights with Chinese men, who if born in the United States were allowed to vote, and Indian men, who under the Dawes Severalty Act had been granted citizenship and the accompanying access of males to the polling places. In a Fourth of July speech, national suffrage organizer Laura M. Johns referred to the enfranchisement of the Nez Pierce Indian men and said she believed "women were as much entitled to privileges of citizenship as those savages."[23]

Disregarding Duniway's dictum that only local people should conduct suffrage campaigns, the Idaho equal suffragists commended Laura M. John's work in Idaho on behalf of the national suffrage association. Then they went on to invite Carrie Chapman Catt, the expert organizer who had perfected her tactics in the Colorado campaign, to visit Idaho during the summer and assist with the final thrust for victory, at which time Helen Young of Wallace reported that Mell Woods had offered to pay twenty-five dollars towards Catt's travel expenses if she would come.

Without waiting for Catt, the Idaho suffragists continued to prepare for the campaign. Eunice Pond Athey, the association's secretary, wrote to prominent businessmen and politicians requesting them to express their views on woman suffrage. Favorable responses were published, and some of the more articulate men, such as the young lawyer and political aspirant William E. Borah, were invited to speak before the 1896 equal suffrage convention to be staged in Boise the first three days of July.[24]

When Carrie Chapman Catt arrived, instructions were issued for the final

Laura M. Johns

assault. Meeting at the state equal suffrage headquarters in Boise on August 20, the suffrage association's advisory board members (Blanche Whitman, association president; Eunice Pond Athey, association secretary; William Balderston, editor of the *Statesman*; James A. McGee, chairman of the Democratic state central committee; and Mr. and Mrs. D. L. Badley) led by Catt prepared a long list of orders to be carried out by the local suffrage clubs. For the final phase of the campaign local suffragists were to select "a representative man from each of the political parties" to serve on their council and act as a contact with men on the "doubtful lists." The advisory board made it clear that "it is better for some reasons that men perform this part of the work [the compiling of the "doubtful lists" then contacting the men on the lists] as many men will talk more frankly to men than to women."[25] In addition to polling the vote, suffrage workers were instructed to solicit endorsements of equal suffrage from politicians and ministers.

On the subject of campaign speakers, the advisory board was insistent that the influence of a male lecturer who "belongs to the same political faith, will reach much farther than that of a straight woman suffrage speaker." They went on to announce: "We shall have but one lady speaker in the campaign, Mrs. Mary C. C. Bradford of Denver. We shall send her to the most doubtful points only."[26] It is likely that Mary Bradford would not have been allowed to deliver any lectures if the Idaho Equal Suffrage Association had not already arranged for her visit and if her expenses were not being paid by her fellow Colorado suffragists. For the minutes of the board meeting where Catt took over show that when "the matter of Mrs. Bradford's coming was discussed [,] Mrs. Catt reported Mrs. Bradford's stay in our State would be limited to six weeks."[27] Though she was not invited by the Idaho suffrage association, Mormon suffragist Emily S. Richards came from Utah to appeal for support of the cause in the southern Idaho communities where the Mormon men had had their franchise restored in 1892.[28] In addition, the Utah suffrage association contributed campaign literature. There were not many suffrage lecturers on the scene, but the *Statesman* carried numerous letters and quotations from people in Wyoming and Utah testifying to the advantages of allowing women to vote and to the moral righteousness of such laws.

Some of the programs outlined by the advisory board bore fruit. Appeals to members of the political conventions were rewarded when all four parties—Populists, Democrats, Republicans, and Silver Republicans—endorsed the woman suffrage amendment. In addition, most of the state's newspapers declared their support. As the campaign for the equal suffrage amendment went forward, the women sponsored two women as candidates for election to the Boise school board. Both the women's right to be elected to the board and women's right to vote in school board elections were challenged. While the discussion continued around the use of the masculine pronoun in state statutes, thirty-three female taxpayers went to the polling places on Labor Day to cast their votes, "but the judges of election. . . refused to allow them to vote. They took their ballots and put them in a separate box." When the male votes were counted the women were soundly defeated but talk of carrying the question of women voting at school elections to the courts ensued. To some the school election affair was just one more "illustration of the absolute necessity for equal suffrage."[29]

As the general election day drew near, elaborate plans were made to secure every possible vote on the suffrage amendment. The question had already been raised as to whether a majority of all the votes cast in the election was required to carry the amendment or if only a majority of those cast on the proposition was sufficient. Since an earlier amendment unrelated to woman suffrage had been declared void on this basis, the suffragists made every effort to see that all voters cast a vote on the amendment. Committees of women were stationed near the polling places with yellow suffrage banners and circulars beseeching men to "Remember the Amendments." Coffee and sandwiches were served; "this to give the Ladies an easier opportunity of approaching the voters on the amendment question."[30]

There were random newspaper articles against woman suffrage which suffragists such as Helen Young tried to counter. But on the whole there was little organized opposition to the suffrage amendment. On election day the amendment carried by almost a two to one vote—12,126 in favor, 6,282 against. William Balderston's tally of the vote in the *Statesman* showed that every county except Custer reported a majority of their votes in favor, and in Custer there were only twenty-five more votes against the amendment than for it. The southeastern Mormon-dominated counties, where Mormon men were now allowed to vote, showed the largest percentages in support of the amendment.

In spite of the apparent approval of the constitutional amendment, the state board of canvassers ruled, as they had done two years earlier on another amendment, that it was defeated because it had not received a majority of all votes cast in the general election, just a majority of those cast on the amendment. Consequently, the contest was carried to the Idaho supreme court by William E. Borah and James H. Hawley on behalf of the equal suffrage association. Both men supported the idea of enfranchising women; in fact, Hawley twenty-six years earlier had been among those legislators who had voted for Dr. Morgan's original woman suffrage bill.[31]

Ultimately, the justices ruled in favor of the amendment, and earned the praise of Susan B. Anthony for being the first judiciary in the nation to give "the broadest and most liberal interpretation possible" on a woman's rights issue rather than the narrowest.[32] Thus Idaho became the fourth state to extend full voting privileges to its female citizens. As a result of their courtroom efforts rendered without compensation, the two young lawyers Borah and Hawley, who respectively would eventually become Idaho's senator and governor, were greatly praised and appreciated by equal suffrage women.

Once the news was out that the Idaho woman suffrage constitutional amendment had been approved by the electorate and had withstood a supreme court test, congratulations poured in, and Idaho became another example. Suffragists from Montana wrote requesting advice on how to conduct the campaign in their

William E. Borah

own state where the state legislature was considering a proposal to amend their constitution to allow the enfranchisement of women.

In what seemed an appropriate honor to the West which now boasted the only four states where women were enfranchised, the National Woman Suffrage Association held its 1897 convention west of the Mississippi River for the first time. The convention site was Des Moines, Iowa.

The fact that the voting men of Idaho had declared in favor of woman suffrage and that the state supreme court had upheld the referendum was acclaimed as a great victory. The following reasons for the success of woman suffrage in Idaho were enumerated at the convention:

> First, the fact that within the state a large colony of people reside who were formerly residents of Utah at the time the women were voting there and who were then converted to the measure; second, the educational and organizational work of national committee; third, the labors of the various branches of the Idaho association; fourth, the political endorsement by all political parties.[33]

The "brave, true men" of Idaho who had voted for woman suffrage were praised, and the delegate from Idaho, Mell Woods, was applauded as she and her mother Emmeline B. Wells of Utah were called to the platform for a "mother and daughter enfranchised" fanfare. Eunice Pond Athey followed with a special report on suffrage activities in Idaho.

As Carrie Chapman Catt reported to the national suffrage association in 1897, the Mormon influence was an important factor in the enfranchisement of Idaho women. Nevertheless, this point has not been stressed in most studies of woman suffrage in Idaho. This may be due in part to the fact that most of what has been published as the official story of suffrage in Idaho was filtered through the personality of Abigail Scott Duniway who often made anti-Mormon statements, and she had aligned herself with the Republicans in Idaho who spearheaded the move to have all Mormons disfranchised. As we have seen, the representative of the Mormon-dominated Oneida county introduced the first legislation in Idaho designed to enfranchise women, and Mormon women from Utah spread the message of equal suffrage among the Mormon women of southern Idaho. In addition, the Idaho representative to the national suffrage association was the Mormon from Wallace, Mell Woods, who intermittently attended the national suffrage conventions from 1897 until the turn of the century when she moved to California. Mell Woods and Helen Young, who was probably a Mormon also, were the two major woman suffrage voices from the northern Shoshone county area. In their account of woman suffrage in Idaho for the multivolume *History of Woman Suffrage*, William Balderston and Eunice Pond Athey reported, "A strong factor in the [1896 suffrage] campaign was the large colony in the Southern part of the State who were residents of Utah when women voted there and who believed in their enfranchisement."[34]

The awareness of woman suffrage in Idaho's Mormon regions is further documented by an examination of the 1890's subscriber list to the *Woman's Journal* which reveals that most of the Idaho women receiving the suffrage journal resided in Montpelier and Wallace. Boise was the third area where there were a few subscribers.[35] Likewise, many of the early officers of the state suffrage association were from Wallace and Montpelier. For nearly one hundred years, from midnineteenth century until the midtwentieth century, Mormons' role in Idaho politics was controversial.[36] For a period in the 1880s Mormon men were not allowed to vote or hold political office in the state. Looking back one might conclude that the association of woman suffrage with Mormons might have hurt the suffrage cause. In 1871 the consideration of a woman suffrage bill ended with a tie vote in the territorial legislature. With that much support it would seem as though the question would be raised in the following years. While it was discussed it did not seem to have much support. It may have been because it was seen as a Mormon issue. The Mormon influence has been stressed here because it has hitherto gone largely undocumented, but there were certainly other forces which also contributed to the realization of the vote for women in Idaho.

In summary, the major forces at work in Idaho which brought about the enfrachisement of women were: The Mormons who had adopted the idea from their association with the enfranchisement of women in Utah and the church's support of the movement; the Populists who in 1894 officially came out in favor of woman suffrage; the Republican party; Abigail Scott Duniway and William Balderston; the reformers associated with the Women's Christian Temperance Union; plus the workers in the local suffrage clubs and national suffragists.

The Idaho constitution could be amended in 1896 to allow women to vote because it seemed an idea whose time had come. Three neighboring states had enfranchised their women and the political sentiment for women's rights led by the Populists was at its highest point. So, many felt Idaho women should be allowed to vote also. If the liquor interests had been as strong or as organized as they were in the Pacific Coast states, Idaho voters would probably not have amended their constitution to accommodate women. As a national suffrage worker observed, "If Idaho had had San Francisco, with all its liquor interests and foreigners banded together, she would probably have been defeated as was California."[37]

Idaho's addition to the triumvirate of full suffrage states caused rejoicing by members of the national suffrage movement in that there was another example to hold up for display. It was the testing and perfecting of methods, however, which national organizers saw as Idaho's most important contribution to the cause. The county organization developed in Colorado had been employed in Idaho with precinct workers going from door-to-door in some areas. This tactic of canvassing voters and educating the public on the suffrage issue, which depended for its effectiveness on the rank and file of the movement, proved to be the operational strategy of the woman's movement for the next quarter century in its continued drive for the enfranchisement of all women. National American Woman Suffrage Association conventioneers in 1897 were told to study these methods and improve them for as they were warned: "Until we do this kind of house-to-house work we can never expect to carry any of the states in which there are large cities."[38]

Notes

[1]T. A. Larson's, "Woman's Rights in Idaho," *Idaho Yesterdays* 16 (Spring 1972):2-19, is the only recent study of early suffrage activities in Idaho. While Abigail Scott Duniway's *Path Breaking* (Portland, Oregon: James, Kerns, and Abbott, 1914) is a detailed contemporary record, it must be taken into account that Duniway had her prejudices and made herself and her point of view most important in her narration of the events. The *History of Woman Suffrage* 4:589-97 has a chapter on the suffrage campaign in Idaho written by two participants—William Balderston and Eunice Pond Athey.

[2]*Idaho Statesman*, 10 January 1871; also see 5 January 1871.

[3]John Hailey, *The History of Idaho* (Boise: Press of Syms-York, 1910), p. 163; Merill D. Beal and Merle W. Wells, *History of Idaho*, 3 vols. (New York: Lewis Historical Publishing Co., 1959), 1:441.

[4]*Idaho Statesman*, 12 February 1870; 25 May; 6 June 1872.

[5]*Idaho Statesman*, 15 May 1886.

[6]*History of Woman Suffrage*, 4:589; also see, pp. 1101-1104.

[7]An article from the *Avalanche* as cited in the *Idaho Democrat*, a Mormon newspaper published in southern Idaho, 24 March 1883.

[8]*Boise City Republican*, 16 October 1886.

[9]*Whisner Leader*, 28 January 1887; also see Beal and Wells, 1:551-611.

[10]*History of Woman Suffrage*, 3:788.

[11]*Mountain Home Bulletin*, 29 October 1888.

[12]*Mountain Home Bulletin*, 6 October 1888.

[13]*Salt Lake Herald*, 28 March 1890.

[14]*History of Woman Suffrage*, 4:943.

[15]*Caldwell Tribune*, 3 October 1891. Some details of the operation of the Women's Christian Temperance Union of Idaho can be found in its minutes and correspondence at the Idaho State Historical Society, Boise, Idaho.

[16]Minutes of the Fifth Annual Convention of the Women's Christian Temperance Union of Idaho held in Boise City, September 25-28, 1891, p. 22.

[17]Unidentified newspaper clipping dateline Boise City, 9 August 1894, Scrapbook, 1891-1901, Anthony Papers.

[18]*History of Woman Suffrage*, 4:590.

[19]Larson, "Woman's Rights in Idaho," p. 9.

[20]Minutes of the First State Suffrage Organization, 20 November 1895. For details of suffrage activities and the names of the participants, see the Equal Suffrage Association of Idaho Minutebook and Letters, Idaho State Historical Society.

[21]As quoted in *Idaho Statesman*, 21 November 1895; also see, Anthony Diary, 18 November 1895.

[22]*Idaho Statesman*, 21 November 1895.

[23]*Caldwell Tribune*, 4 July 1896; also see, "Equal Suffragists' Desires" in the Equal Suffrage Association of Idaho file.

[24]Mrs. M. C. Athey to W. E. Borah, 4-11 June 1896, William E. Borah Papers; Mrs. M. C. Athey to James H. Hawley, 4 June 1896, James H. Hawley Papers; 4 July 1896 minutes of the Equal Suffrage Association of Idaho, all at the Idaho State Historical Society.

[25]Equal Suffrage Association of Idaho Minutebook, 20 August 1896.

[26]Ibid.

[27]Ibid.

[28]*History of Woman Suffrage*, 4:592-93; Beal and Wells, 2:84.

[29]*Idaho Statesman*, 8 September 1896; also see 3, 6, 13 September 1896.

[30]Equal Suffrage Association of Idaho Minutebook, 2 July 1896.

[31]James H. Hawley to Mrs. M. C. Athey, 20 July 1896, Hawley Papers.

[32]Harper, *Anthony*, 3:918-19.

[33]*Des Moines* (Iowa) *Leader*, 29 January 1897.

[34]*History of Woman Suffrage*, 4:592-93. In his study of women's rights in Idaho, T. A. Larson cites the Mormon influence in the suffrage fight and notes that he could not determine if Joseph Morgan was a church member. In my study I found evidence that the Mormons influenced the Idaho campaign. In addition I found evidence that Mormons who emigrated to Canada to avoid persecution under the Edmunds-Tucker Bill may have been instrumental in initiating the move for woman suffrage and the move to allow married women the right to hold property in their own names in Canada. The time and place is right to explain "the prairie provinces' liberal attitude towards women," cited by Catherine Lyle Cleverdon *The Woman Suffrage Movement in Canada* (Toronto: University of Toronto Press, 1950).

[35]National American Woman Suffrage Association, Subject File, Box 78, Library of Congress Manuscript Division.

[36]Boyd A. Marlin, "Idaho: The Sectional State" in *Politics in the American West* edited by Frank H. Jones (Salt Lake City: University of Utah Press, 1969): 195-96.

[37]*History of Woman Suffrage*, 4:293.

[38]Ibid.

VIII. FOUR EXPERIMENTS EXAMINED

It is probably true that the ballot and its attendant circumstances have increased the unhealthy restlessness of some women, and have left profoundly unmoved many others; but between these two extremes there are indubitably a large class who have been awakened to a great practical interest in problems confronting the social body, and who are beginning to understand more of that patriotism which does not talk but acts. Hitherto, at least, the predictions of extremists have been confuted, for the ballot in the hands of woman has neither unsexed her nor regenerated the world.

William Macleod Raine
As quoted in *Deseret News*
February 13, 1902

Many of the predictions of both advocates and opponents of woman suffrage were not fulfilled in the four states of Wyoming, Utah, Colorado, and Idaho where women voted at the end of the nineteenth century. When the practical results of enfranchisement were studied by the National American Woman Suffrage Association in 1902, the well-known Western novelist William Macleod Raine reported that from his observations, especially in Colorado, he had concluded that since women had been allowed to vote, there seemed to be cleaner streets, more equitable laws governing property rights, improvement of parks, and better care of female prisoners. On the other hand, he felt that having women at the polls had made voting more cumbersome. As he summed it up, access to the polling booths had not unsexed women; on the other hand, women had not used the ballot to regenerate the world.[1]

In 1906 the editor of the *Deseret News* observed that in the experiment with equal suffrage in the four Rocky Mountain states the promised purification had "not panned out to any very extraordinary extent"; moreover, partisanship had "taken hold of the lady voters with equal if not greater force than" it had influenced men.[2] The same year the New York Collegiate Equal Suffrage League sponsored a study of woman suffrage in Colorado and found that few women sought public office in that equal suffrage state, and when they did, women voters tended to vote along party rather than feminist lines. In short, as one Colorado woman phrased it: "They vote with men, and for men, and just about like men."[3]

A writer for *Pearson's Magazine* rhetorically asked, "What Women Have Done with Votes?" Then answered, Nothing—"nothing revolutionary, startling, uplifting, or sensational."[4] On the other hand, some observers insisted that women's involvement in politics in these four Western states had resulted in more calm and order at polling places, in the selection of candidates of higher moral character, in better schools, in more moral and sanitary legislation, and in making "intemperance and other bad habits unpopular." Finally, there was little evidence

136

that women voted from a feminist point of view or that they were using the ballot to bring about changes in what was referred to as "women's sphere."

Promoters of the idea of woman suffrage gathered data on the four states in an attempt to demonstrate the positive impact of woman suffrage. Too often, however, they concluded that all things defined as good were a direct result of women having political power. For example, an Oregon equal suffrage tract published in 1906 used census data to show that in the states where women voted, wages and population had increased and agricultural and manufacturing interests had grown. In drawing these conclusions, variables other than woman suffrage were ignored and an attempt was made to draw a direct correlation between the states' growth factors and women's right to vote.

Critics of woman suffrage also examined the experiments in the four Rocky Mountain states. Most often it was the Utah, or the Mormon, example which they attacked. From its formation in 1830 on through most of the nineteenth century the Mormon church was viewed with suspicion because it very effectively used its religious organization for political purposes. After the Civil War the concern with the Mormons and their practice of plural marriage became a national concern. Polygamy was seen as the last of the "twin relics of barbarism" and there were those who felt the federal government should take action to crush it as slavery had been eliminated. National pressure was such that the Mormons offically abandoned the plural marriage practice in 1890.

In 1893 Kate Field used polygamy as an argument against enfranchising women. In 1902, in a general attack on women voting which insinuated that all women were thoughtless and ignorant, Grover Cleveland, who during his Presidency eight years earlier had approved the Utah statehood constitution which included a woman suffrage clause, now pointed to Utah as proof that the influence of women in politics was "neither elevating or refining." As evidence he noted the character of the men elected to the United States Senate from Utah. Antisuffrage tracts often dismissed the enfranchisement of women in Wyoming, Utah, Idaho, and Colorado, asserting that the Mormons held the balance of political power in all four states, thus eliminating separation of church and state. It was concluded, therefore, that the additional force of women voters in these states only aided a political majority which was "not only un-American regarding our governmental ideals but anti-American."[5] During this period there were a few Mormons in Wyoming and Colorado; about one fourth of Idaho's population was associated with the church; and in Utah the population base was predominantly Mormon.

Suffragists themselves persisted in questioning the legitimacy of the experiment in Utah. These doubts were frequently fired by suffrage women from Utah who contended that Mormon women voted only as directed. This explanation was developed on an international scene when a Utah woman told a suffrage audience in Berlin in 1904 that Utah women had the ballot, but they had no freedom of choice.[6] As a historian of the woman suffrage movement, Ida Husted Harper observed in 1916, "So bitter is the feeling against polygamy, which is all Utah represents to the average individual, that the suffrage leaders have been practically barred from citing this State as a satisfactory example."[7]

Antisuffragists held up the child labor laws and divorce rates in the four equal suffrage states to show that the ballot in the hands of women did not improve the world. In addition, critics carefully watched registration and voting participation in the full suffrage states to see if interest lagged once woman suffrage was no longer a novelty. What they found was that women's interest, like that of men, varied and was much lower than was optimal in a democratic system. They did find, however, that women were generally more concerned than men when it came to local issues and school elections. As Colorado Governor McIntyre said, "The women have voted in as large a proportion as the men." In a 1911 article in *The Independent,* Ida Husted Harper reported on the Idaho experience, saying women constituted forty-two percent of the population and by the offcial statistics they cast forty percent of the vote in Boise and over thirty-five percent in the rest of the state.[8]

While the Utah example was most often faulted, the Wyoming experience was the best known, longest tested, and most often cited. Colorado was considered to be the most reliable test because of that state's large population and urban center. Idaho, on the other hand, was the least known; consequently, it was seldom used as a point of reference.

In 1879 a Mr. Courtney introduced the question of woman suffrage to the British Parliament, noting the good effect of suffrage in Wyoming. For documentation he quoted a letter from the speaker of the Wyoming House of Representatives who summarized his praise of woman suffrage saying: "Women are more interested in good government and its moral influence upon our future sons and daughters than men. They look above and beyond mere party questions or influences in deciding their vote."[9] A large number of the testimonies regarding the operation of woman suffrage in the West were generated as a result of inquiries such as Mr. Courtney's from other states or countries, debates conducted in magazines such as *Outlook,* the annual suffrage association examination of the state of suffrage affairs, and Susan B. Anthony's request that the friends of woman suffrage "write out every good happening and everything said by any prominent person in favor of woman suffrage and keep something of the sort floating around in the papers all the time."[10]

At the turn of the century, Idaho Governor Frank Steunenberg made it clear in a *Harper's Bazaar* article that he considered the experiment with woman suffrage a success in his state. Another Idaho governor was quoted in 1904 as saying: "The extension of the franchise of the women of Idaho has positively purified its politics. . . . It has also taken politics out of the saloon to a great extent and has elevated it, especially local politics, to a higher plane."[11] As we have seen, Wyoming governors were particularly famous for declaring in the strongest terms in favor of the experiment in their state.

At the same 1902 suffrage convention where William Macleod Raine proclaimed that woman suffrage in the West had neither unsexed women nor reformed the world, Emmeline B. Wells denied accusations that Mormon women did not participate in politics, and as evidence to the contrary she pointed to the fact that Mormon women composed the entire delegation to the convention. She insisted the influence of women had been "distinctly elevating" and since the women vote was a "a terror to the evil doers" the course therefore was "upward and onward."[12]

The former Utah Senator, F. J. Cannon, admitted that his skepticism had vanished, and now he was thoroughly convinced that women with the ballot would not "degrade politics."[13] Even Fred J. Kiesel, who had avidly opposed including women in the electorate during the constitutional convention period in Utah, seven years later could graciously admit "women can be trusted." Saying his original fears had been mistaken, Kiesel acknowledged that in his own household he supported the Democratic party while the female members of his family consistently voted Republican.[14]

The fact that women were allowed to vote did not seem to result in the shattering of domestic relations, and examples of husbands and wives of opposing political persuasions were frequently spotlighted. As Utah's governor, Heber M. Wells, noted, women could vote and still remain in their sphere. Another Utah governor, John C. Cutler, concluded that giving women the vote was a good move, saying "So far as I am able to judge, Utah has suffered none of the misfortunes which the enemies of equal suffrage predict but on the contrary has been materially benefited by giving the women a 'square deal.' "[15]

Woman suffrage is usually viewed by historians as a middle class reform movement in the United States; this view holds in the early experiments in the West. Most leaders and supporters of the movement in the four Rocky Mountain states were white, middle class, Protestant, conservers of the community. Prominent social, political, and religious leaders were often supporters of the idea of allowing women political rights. It was reported that the leading women in Denver were enthusiastic advocates of the suffrage movement; in fact, "it has been told far and wide of the meetings of the Denver Suffragists, that wherever they are assembled together no loafers congregate nor women who are not intelligent and respectable."[16] There was some identification of woman suffrage with temperance and Populism, but generally, woman suffrage in the American West was not a movement led by people who sought to overthrow or even radically reform the established social-economic system. Even in the cases where the Populist party was a prime force in bringing about woman suffrage, the women tended to vote for the more moderate Republican party. The evidence indicates that most Western women were generally conservative in their political views and in their defense of tradition, especially when it came to championing the standard roles of wife and mother.

Among the woman suffrage advocates, there was a disproportionately large percentage of women medical doctors. While Dr. Alida C. Avery was a prominent early leader of the movement in Colorado, three physicians—Ellen B. Ferguson,

Romania B. Pratt, and Mattie Hughes Cannon—were active in woman suffrage in Utah. If such women chose to disseminate ideas and influence other women, their role as educated medical advisors made them very influential. Like medical doctors, women lawyers comprised a disproportionate segment of women's rights workers. Generally, professional women in the nineteenth century West were advocates of woman suffrage.

Regardless of professional background, proponents of woman suffrage, as well as opponents, often manifested racist attitudes. Arguments for granting women political rights in the last quarter of the nineteenth century were often based on racist assumptions. As the argument went: Native born, white women should not be the political inferiors of black men, Oriental men, or Indian men. Since the white women were generally better educated and often owned property, they should be permitted to vote if black men were. The emotional arguments continued in this tone. As we have seen, the enfranchisement of freedmen inflamed many equal rights workers, and the appeal used by some politicians that "my wife" or "my mother" is surely as good as a black man was provocative. The cry of white women's superiority to Indians and Chinese had a special appeal in the American West. On the other hand, an often heard emotional condemnation against enfranchising women was that it would not only be white women who voted, but black women, Chinese women, and Indian women could not be kept from the polls if woman suffrage became a reality. Opponents made it clear that they felt that these women were less worthy and less eligible to vote than their male counterparts. Many politicians openly acknowledged that they were opposed to allowing, what we would refer to today as minority men, political privileges, but they were even more determined that similar rights would not be extended to minority women whom they felt free to refer to in the most loathsome terms.

Many pioneer woman suffragists who had fought for the abolition of slavery and had worked in the Reconstruction years for universal equal rights regardless of color or sex were angry when freedmen were enfranchised and they were denied the same rights. But racist arguments were not a major theme of the suffrage movement so long as the women held to the liberal principle of inalienable human rights. It was only in the last decade of the century that the atmosphere changed. When social Darwinian concepts which made racist views of humanity intellectually acceptable, woman suffragists were not exempt. The woman's movement was undergoing many changes, one of which was the use of racist arguments to further its cause. The general anti-Chinese sentiment in the West and the granting of citizenship with its accompanying voting rights to some Indian men under the 1887 allotment program made it easy to appeal to Westerners' racism. As we have seen, this ploy was frequently used by woman suffragists and their friends and foes.

What other factors then contributed to the fact that in the last quarter of the nineteenth century Western men were willing to grant political privilege to the women of these four Rocky Mountain states? The societies were less rigid; they were still in a state of transformation; and lawmakers felt that they had little to lose and possibly a great deal of publicity to gain by granting women the vote. Moreover, the experiment in the four states showed that woman suffrage did not make a discernible difference in the outcome of elections.

In the period 1868 to 1896—from the close of the Civil War to the eve of the Spanish American War—the franchise was extended in the American West. Easterners traveled west on the newly completed transcontinental railroad to see the frontier, and suffrage lecturers toured the region, stimulating interest in the idea of enfranchising women. Thus territorial legislatures considered granting women the ballot as a means to promote their regions.

In 1869 and 1870 the territorial status of Wyoming and Utah made it easier to achieve woman suffrage because a bill approved by the territorial legislature and signed by the governor was all that was necessary. On the other hand, the territorial status complicated the matter because the territorial governors were appointed by the President and were usually considered outsiders and often political opponents by the citizenry and the territorial legislatures. For example, in Wyoming when the woman suffrage legislation was first discussed, it was viewed as a means to embarrass the governor by putting him in the position of having to declare in favor of woman suffrage by signing the bill or allowing himself to go on record against it by vetoing the bill. Either way the governor moved there were those politicians who could use the issue to ridicule him.

Similar circumstances occurred in Utah when the territorial legislature passed legislation allowing women to hold office. As George Q. Cannon said, the legislature could afford to pass the bill and thus gain support of Eastern suffragists, but Utahns probably would not have to live with the problem because the governor would veto it. Ultimately, they would have a political victory over the governor and no real change in the status quo. The territorial governors were in an awkward position on the subject of woman suffrage for no matter what they did it could be used against them. For example, in 1870 the territorial governor of Colorado, Edward M. McCook, urged the legislature to extend suffrage to the women, but the legislators voted down the measure, saying they would not be dictated to by federal officials. There was also the factor that the governor was appointed by Republican President Grant, while the territorial legislature was dominated by Democrats.

Even if suffrage was achieved under territorial status, it was limited by the fact that territorial residents do not vote for the President of the United States or for their own governors. Their vote is limited to elections within the territory, or in other words, those for the representatives to the territorial legislature and local officials. However, because woman suffrage would have such limited effects, people were more willing to test it in a territory. In addition, they knew that the issue would have to be reconsidered when the territory entered the union; since in order to achieve statehood, a constitution specifying voter qualifications would have to be presented for the approval of the territorial electorate and the national Congress. On the other hand, the territorial status proved to be a negative factor for woman suffrage when Congress exercised control of the territories by legislatively revoking woman suffrage in Utah. Wyoming's bid for statehood was threatened because of its constitutional clause enfranchising women. Moreover, when Colorado and Idaho applied for statehood, the argument that inclusion of a provision for woman suffrage endangered their proposed statehood proved very persuasive; consequently, such a clause was not included. In the Utah debate this argument was also heard; nevertheless, after a long battle woman suffrage was included largely because of the Mormon church's long-time support of the idea.

The relative ease whereby woman suffrage could be realized in the West should not be overlooked. Granting women access to the ballot was certainly easier in Wyoming than it would have been in Massachusetts, for example. First, the territorial status of the region only required that the legislature and the governor approve the measure; a vote of support from the total electorate was not necessary. Even in the two states—Colorado and Idaho—where the vote was granted by altering the constitution by popular vote it was still easier than it would have been in the East. Moreover, the groundwork had been done when their constitutions were originally written.

One rather romantic explanation of why woman suffrage was a reality in the American West at the end of the nineteenth century was as follows:

> Suffrage had come to them in the tops of the Rocky Mountains largely because their state was young, it gloried in its youth, and wanted to celebrate by seizing a growing issue and making it a matter in which wisdom and precedent would trickle down from the mountain-tops to the parched and arid political plains below.[17]

Certainly, there were liberal, equalitarian-minded individuals in the West who supported woman suffrage, but enfranchisement became an actuality as a result of expediency, often temporary expediency which was afterwards parlayed into a virtue and used as a promotional gimmick. Motives behind the enfranchisement of women in the Rocky Mountain West were usually conservative, political motives, not progressive, ideological ones based on equalitarian thought, though the advocates often phrased their arguments in the liberal rhetoric of the day. There is evidence to indicate that legislators and governors who were responsible for passage of such legislation in the early years were confident of the basic conservatism of the women. There was little fear that the Western women would use the ballot to reform society or to seize political power. There was not much danger, because, with the exception of Utah, there were not many women.[18] Moreover, Western women were not organized and pushing to change society as was the case in some Eastern states. By the 1890s there were some Women's Christian Temperance organizations in the areas, but they were not considered a serious threat.

During the last three decades of the century, the West was going through a period of change. Railroads had ended the isolation, the frontier was closing, and territorial status was being traded for statehood. In the process of writing constitutions and preparing themselves for self-governance, the Westerners had to consciously think through and vote on a form of government which included a definition of the electorate. Established East Coast areas did not have this opportunity.

Almost by definition Westerners were promoters in those days of boosterism; so it was natural that they would seize upon such a nonthreatening scheme as enfranchising women as a means to publicize their region and hopefully attract settlers, investors, or supporters in their bids for statehood. Even if advertising was not the initial motive in granting women the ballot, once woman suffrage became a reality in a region, it was used to make the area known. Numerous governors from the four equal suffrage areas offered favorable testimony as to the impact of women voting in their territory or state.

In the last three decades of the nineteenth century, the numerous minor political parties were usually supportive of the idea of women's rights. Their appeal was as much to a new constituency as it was to women voting in terms of principle. In the case of the Populists, the fact that the women's organizations were willing to support the free coinage of silver enhanced their image with the party which in turn was a very important factor in Colorado in women gaining the vote in 1893. Populists were also important in the suffrage contest in Idaho. Most important was the traditionally third party role that they played in introducing woman suffrage as a political issue, thus making it necessary for the two major parties to deal with it. Ultimately, however, this force in support of woman suffrage was lost when the Populist party was absorbed by the Democrats which had been the party most resistant to women's rights.

On the other hand, since the Civil War the national Republican party had generally supported or at least paid lip service to the woman's cause. In Wyoming it was the Republican governor and other federal officials who defended woman suffrage when a Democratic legislature tried to revoke it. Moreover, at the time of its entrance into the union, Wyoming was considered to be a Republican state. In Utah the original supporters of woman suffrage, the Godbeites, first gravitated towards the national Republican party but ended up as Populists. Most Utah women who had been long-time advocates of woman suffrage, with the notable exceptions of Emma J. McVicker, Charlotte Ives Cobb Godbe Kirby, and Emmeline B. Wells, opted for the Democratic party when the territory divided along Democratic-Republican lines. However, when the Democrats claimed their party had bestowed the franchise on women, the Republicans reminded them, alluding to Brigham Robert's oratorical feats, that four-fifths of the time in the constitutional convention devoted to arguing against woman suffrage was used by Democrats. In Idaho, the Republican party and affiliated newspapers tended to be early equal suffrage advocates; later Populists were strong supporters of woman suffrage in Idaho.

Reporting that the women of Colorado and Utah voted for William Jennings Bryan and thus the Democrats in 1896 and those of Wyoming for the Republicans,

Harper's Weekly summarized the women's relationship to political parties in the following manner:

> Female suffrage owes its establishment to the Populist party, assisted in a lesser degree by the Republican party. As a rule the straight Democrats have been opposed to allowing the women to vote.[19]

With this kind of party breakdown of support for woman suffrage and alignment with political parties, it is logical that the militant Congressional Union for Woman Suffrage, led by Alice Paul, which broke from the National American Woman Suffrage Association in 1914 to demand passage of the federal amendment, decided to apply pressure to Woodrow Wilson's Democratic administration and Democrats in Congress by actively campaigning against Democratic candidates, especially those in the equal suffrage states. [20] It is also not surprising that they met the greatest opposition to such tactics in Utah where a majority of dedicated suffragists also had become dedicated Democrats.

Without a doubt, it had been a Democratic-dominated legislature which had originally granted the women the ballot in Wyoming; however, they were Democratic more because of their opposition to the Republican-appointed territorial officials than on the basis of political philosophy or alignment with the national party. Yet the Republican party had traditionally been identified with human rights and the creation of the Fourteenth and Fifteenth amendments which had involved the federal government in the definition of the electorate, while the Democrats, especially those in the South, persisted in believing that spelling out voter qualifications was exclusively a prerogative of the states. As had been the case in Kansas, the Republicans chose to be silent on the subject of woman suffrage in their effort to get black men enfranchised; but the Democrats unequivocally declared against both black and female enfranchisement.

The fact that the Republicans permitted Laura de Force Gordon and Susan B. Anthony to sit on the speakers' platform at the 1872 convention but refused to allow them to speak was symbolic of the extent of the party's commitment to woman suffrage. And even this concession, along with the vague party platform which declared woman's demands for rights were worthy of respectful consideration, disappeared from future party conventions. On the national or local scene, woman suffrage was not generally a party issue. No major party in the nineteenth century consistently and unequivocally supported the idea of enfranchising women.

While politicians often did not support the enfranchisement of women, it was brewers and liquor interests who pushed the vigorous campaign against woman suffrage. Despite the fact that none of the states where women were enfranchised in the nineteenth century passed prohibition legislation, fear that women would succeed in making liquor illegal continued to grow. These fears were fired in 1883 when the Women's Christian Temperance Union organized a Laramie, Wyoming, chapter of women pledged, as they said, to use their "sacred weapon, the ballot," to do their utmost "in creating a higher public sentiment against the manufacture and sale of alcoholic beverages."[21] They were successful in getting the issue on the ballot in Laramie the next year. The temperance measure was defeated, but nearly 500 votes had been cast in its favor. As the Women's Christian Temperance Union became stronger throughout the nation and the National Woman Suffrage Association talked more and more in terms of using the vote to purify society and politics, the brewers, who had consolidated their production operations and doubled the production of beer in the 1880s, tended to be much more assertive in fighting the enfranchisement referendums and in disseminating literature against woman suffrage.

In spite of some people's fears, the fact that women voted in the four Rocky Mountain states made little difference in the social, economic, or political condition of women in those areas. Few women were elected to public office nor were they invited into the backrooms where political decisions were made. The only change effected by female suffrage, other than women's psychological feeling of participation, was that candidates for public office had their moral character more carefully examined and behavior at polling places was generally more decorous on election day. Finally, there were few social reforms or improvements in women's status nor was there much purification of politics. As Theodore Roosevelt summarized the impact of woman suffrage in a letter to Lyman Abbot, published in 1909 in the antisuffrage newspaper *Remonstrance:*

> I am unable to see that there has been any special improvement in the position of women in those states in the West that have adopted it. I do not think that giving the women suffrage will produce any marked improvement in the conduct of women. I do not believe that it will produce any of the evils feared.[22]

Many astute suffragists really did not expect that woman suffrage would change the world; they argued for it simply because it was a symbol of justice and equality in what was purported to be a democratic society based on the consent of the governed. As a writer in the *Revolution* in 1870 had predicted:

> The ballot...will achieve for women no more than it has achieved for man.... The ballot is only a crust—a crumb.... But woman's chief discontent is not with her political, but with her social, and particularly with her marital bondage.[23]

As the women's movement entered the twentieth century, this central liberal principle of natural rights and critiques of the family structure were both set aside, and the new generation of suffragists focused solely on the ballot. They persisted in promoting the vote as the means to rid society of evils, not as a symbol of equality. In so doing, they had to ignore the evidence that equal suffrage did not radically alter society or women's roles in it. This shift from arguments of natural rights and justice to those of the vote as a means to reform was made in spite of the fact that the experiences in the four full suffrage Western states did not support their doctrine.

Notes

[1] *Deseret News,* 13 February 1902.

[2] *Deseret News* editorial, 12 October 1906.

[3] Priscilla Leonard, "Woman Suffrage in Colorado," *Outlook,* 55 (March 2, 1897):791.

[4] Ike Russel, "What Women Have Done with Votes," *Pearson's Magazine* [n.d.], p. 538, clipping in Church Archives.

[5] Grace Duffield Goodwin, *Anti-Suffrage: Ten Good Reasons* (New York: Duffield, 1913), pp. 110-11.

[6] Speech by Mrs. C. E. Allen before the International Woman's Congress in Berlin, June 1904, as reported to the Church Presidency by Lydia D. Alder, Church Archives.

[7] *Brooklyn Daily Eagle,* published sometime in 1916 and clipped for the Ida Harper Scrapbook, 1898-1926, Manuscript Division, New York Public Library Annex.

[8] Ida Husted Harper, "Woman Suffrage in Six States," *The Independent* 71 (November 2, 1911):969.

[9] Millicent G. Fawcett, in Theodore Stanton, ed., The Woman Question in Europe (reprint of 1884 edition, New York: Source Book Press, 1971), p. 28.

[10] Harper, *Anthony,* 3:1203.

[11] *Harper's Bazaar,* clipping and unidentified newspaper clipping in Scrapbook, 1902-1904, Anthony Papers.

[12] *Salt Lake Herald,* 17 February 1902.

[13] *Deseret News,* 14 February 1902.

[14] *Boston Transcript* as quoted in *Deseret News,* 10 March 1902.

[15] *Morning Oregonian,* 31 May 1906.

[16] "About Women," *Jenness Miller Monthly* 7 (July 1894):13.

[17] Russell, p. 538.

[18] The census data for 1870 indicates that when woman suffrage was being considered in the four territories the population was approximately 9,000 in Wyoming, 87,000 in Utah, 40,000 in Colorado, and 15,000 in Idaho. Utah was the only place where women represented nearly half of the total; in the other territories women composed one-fourth, or less, of the population.

[19]*Harper's Weekly* 44 (October 6, 1900):950.

[20]Inez Irwin, *The Story of the Women's Party* (New York: Harcourt, Brace, 1921; reprint ed., New York: Kraus, 1971), p. 89.

[21]*Laramie Sentinal*, 1 December 1883.

[22]*Remonstrance*, January 1909.

[23]*Revolution*, 27 October 1870.

IX. THE NADIR OF WOMAN SUFFRAGE

At the National American Woman Suffrage Association convention in 1896, Susan B. Anthony in her opening remarks summarized the past quarter of a century of suffrage activity. She said:

> The thought that brought us here twenty-eight years ago was that, if the Federal Constitution could be invoked to protect black men in the right to vote, the same great authority could be invoked to protect women. The question has been urged upon every Congress since 1869. We asked at first for a Sixteenth Amendment enfranchising women; then for suffrage under the Fourteenth Amendment; then, when the Supreme Court had decided that against us, we returned to the Sixteenth Amendment and have pressed it ever since. The same thing has been done in this Fifty-fourth Congress which has been done in every Congress for a decade, namely, the introducing of a bill providing for the new amendment....

> You will notice that the seats of the delegation from Utah are marked by a large United States flag bearing three stars, a big one and two smaller ones. The big star is for Wyoming, because it stood alone for a quarter of a century as the only place where women had full suffrage. Colorado comes next, because it is the first State where a majority of the men voted to grant women equal rights. Then comes Utah, because its men in convention assembled—in spite of the bad example of Congress, which took the right away from its women nine years ago—those men, having seen the good effects of woman suffrage for years, voted by an overwhelming majority to leave out the little word "male" from the suffrage clause of their new State Constitution, and their action was ratified by the electors. Next year, if I am here, I hope to rejoice with you over woman suffrage in California and Idaho.[1]

Within the year, Susan B. Anthony did get to rejoice over the enfranchisement of women in Idaho, but it would be fifteen years before suffragists would be able to celebrate success in California. By then Anthony would be dead. In 1896 it seemed as though the suffrage movement was really underway; that autumn Idaho voters approved the amendment of their state constitution and suffrage workers were canvassing California hoping for a similar result. But the "liquor combine," as Anthony called it, was victorious in California.

Historians often label the period from 1896 to 1910 as the doldrum years for woman suffrage because no additional states enfranchised their female citizens during this period and the campaign for a federal amendment languished. As we have seen, arrival at this nadir was not a sudden event. Congress' passage of the Edmunds-Tucker Bill taking the ballot from the women of Utah Territory in 1887 and the Senate's two to one vote the same year defeating the Anthony

148

The Apotheosis of Liberty
National American Woman Suffrage Convention, 1896

amendment the first time it came to a vote were omens tending to demoralize the National Woman Suffrage Association which soon began merger negotiations with the American Association.

Why did the woman suffrage movement sink into doldrums after 1896? Part of the answer may be that since the successes in the Rocky Mountain West had had little to do with an ideology of equality or an effective, enduring suffrage movement, what appeared to be a suffrage tide quickly subsided once an effective opposition appeared in the form of the antisuffrage association and saloon protective leagues. Once the opposition was organized, it was no longer so easy to use the enfranchisement of women as an advertisement gimmick or as a political ploy against the opposition. Nor was it easy to convince male voters to amend their states' constitutions.

Moreover, the frontier was closed. Improved transportation and communication had made Easterners more familiar with the American West; consequently, they became less inclined to romanticize the West and view it as a region for testing utopian schemes. Most of the West, except for the Southwest and Oklahoma, had been admitted as states. Most of the Western states had written their constitutions, and like the East, the constitutional amendment process was not needed to redefine the electorate.

Also the mood of Americans had changed. In the heyday of Radical Republicanism in the post Civil War era, when the idea of enfranchising women in the territories had first been discussed and the women of the Wyoming and Utah territories had been granted admittance to polling places, liberal equalitarian arguments had held some sway. However, during the final three decades of the nineteenth century the appeal of humanitarian, equalitarian arguments was eroded by the naturalistic view of the life which sanctioned inequality. The sympathy for equality which had been forceful during the Reconstruction Era when the Fourteenth and Fifteenth amendments were adopted had given way to the concept of a restricted ballot, until in 1896 with the Plessy v. Ferguson Supreme Court decision, inequality became constitutional.

Moreover, there was a general reaction against change and experimental schemes, especially those related to the family and sex roles. This conservativism was further manifested in movements such as Comstockery and Purity Crusade. The nation moved to a more conservative social and political stance, marked by the 1886 violent reaction to the labor demonstration in Chicago's Haymarket Square. The suffrage movement modified itself also.

The national suffragists' experience with the question of woman suffrage in Utah helped to move them closer to what is referred to as the Victorian Compromise and a preoccupation with the franchise. The National Woman Suffrage Association, which had been the most critical of the monogamous marital system, had been pressured not to allow the organization to be used by Victoria Woodhull to promote free love or by Belva Lockwood to defend the Mormon women in words often interpreted as a defense of plural marriage. Even Elizabeth Cady Stanton's views on divorce were not generally accepted. This suffrage organization was discredited in conservative days because of its identification with the nontraditional family structure and critiques of monogamous marriage. Faced with attacks from all sides if they attempted to analyze the traditional family structure, women's rights advocates tended to confine themselves more and more to one subject—the vote. Suffrage became the panacea. Thus a feminist ideology of woman's role in society, which would might have resulted in a much greater change in society than woman suffrage produced, was not forthcoming.

After the unification of the two suffrage organizations, equalitarian arguments within the suffrage movement were no longer emphasized; the assumed moral superiority of women came to the fore. In the early days of the movement, Elizabeth Cady Stanton and Susan B. Anthony had argued the case for female participation in the political life of the nation on the basis of natural human rights. Later in the nineteenth century, when Carrie Chapman Catt emerged as leader of the movement, the arguments shifted to focus on the unique insights of women and the supposed purifying impact that would result from female participation in politics. The suffragists attempted to turn the Victorian cult of true womanhood to their advantage. Women did not insist that they were equal to men but focused on how they were unique, especially in the moral realm.

The idea that women's interests differed from those of the rest of the electorate frightened some segments of the society and resulted in the formation of aggressive antisuffrage organizations often backed by brewers who feared prohibition. This resistance to votes for women was based on fears, confirmed by the suffragists' own promotional literature, which advertised that women would likely use the ballot to reform society, especially to eliminate "demon rum"; moreover, they would ignore the persuasion of political bosses. In short, if women were allowed to vote they would naturally use their political power to purify society and clean up politics because, according to the ethic of the day, women were the morally superior sex. Consequently, it was assumed by many, including promoters of woman suffrage, that the bright light of womanly purity and virtue could raise anything, even men and politics, to a more Godly level.

After the merger of the two suffrage associations which was completed in 1890, the second generation of suffragists began to take over as Susan Anthony and Lucy Stone gradually stepped side. This new generation tended to concentrate more on the ballot than on a general critique of woman's role in the society. In addition, the association moved further in the direction of advocating individual state action as supported by the Boston group and away from Anthony's idea of a national constitutional amendment. No longer was there constant pressure on Congress through committee hearings or by lobbying. At Alice Stone Blackwell's suggestion, the suffrage association only convened in Washington, D. C., on alternate years. As Anthony had feared, hopes for a federal amendment faded; after 1893 no Congressional committee gave it a favorable report, thus it disappeared as a national political issue until 1913.

Carrie Chapman Catt 1896

The character of the woman suffrage movement was further altered when a number of Eastern suffrage leaders who had been active in the promotion of woman suffrage in the West left the movement. For example, Phoebe Couzins and Belva Lockwood, two prominent women lawyers, withdrew from the movement. After a number of years devoted to the Populist party, Couzins renounced woman suffrage in 1897 and ultimately became a lobbyist for the United Brewers Association; while Lockwood turned her attention to Indian claims cases and the international peace movement.

It was not only that the suffrage organization was weakened, but antisuffragists, in addition to the brewers and businessmen who profited from the sale of liquor, were beginning to organize and campaign in earnest. Like the suffrage movement, the antimovement was international. The well-known British novelist, Mrs. Humphry Ward, presented a "solemn protest" against woman suffrage before Parliament in 1889. Her petition had force in that it was signed by many women who were identified with liberalism and socialism and would later become supporters of suffrage—Beatrice Webb, Mrs. Creighton, Mrs. T. H. Green, and Mrs. A. Toynbee. Arguing that women had municipal suffrage but should not be granted the right to vote for members of Parliament, Mrs. Humphry Ward spoke for the petitioners saying, "We believe the emancipating process has now reached the limits fixed by the physical constitution of women."[2] In addition, antisuffrage publications such as *The Nineteenth Century* began to popularize the argument against women voting.

Other opponents of woman suffrage argued that women were too frail, too pure, too noble to participate in the political arena. The underlying concern here was that women really would try to purify the often corrupt politics of the Gilded Age. Others feared, or at least said they feared, that women voters would force overly. rigorous social reforms, especially in the area of liquor production and sales. One of the most significant oppositions to feminism in this period, as we have seen, came from those who feared an attack on the monogamous marriage and the traditional nuclear family structure which seemed to be taking place along with urbanization and industrialization at the end of the nineteenth century.

The national woman suffrage organization was further weakened by the fact that the areas where women were allowed to vote did not adequately support the suffrage movement elsewhere. The financial reports of the National American Woman Suffrage Association reveal that the four Rocky Mountain states where women voted were not funding the national association for the years 1895 through 1897. Wyoming's suffrage organization was not even listed as paying dues; Colorado suffragists paid two dollars or less for two years; Utah members contributed thirty-one dollars in 1895, the year when its constitution was being drafted, and nothing in the other two years; while the only listing for Idaho was a forty dollar figure for 1896 which was marked delinquent. While the state organizations of Massachusetts and New York were each putting one hundred to two hundred dollars into the association coffers annually to underwrite campaigns, usually conducted in the West, the four areas where women were being enfranchised only participated when the subject was under consideration in their region.

Moreover, woman suffrage in the Rocky Mountain West had not come about as a direct result of the suffrage movement. The post Civil War climate of equalitarianism initiated the move towards admitting women to political participation and, as we have seen, the suffrage movement was used to promote other goals. While the two constitution writing efforts in Wyoming and Utah were conducted in the midst of some expression of women's sentiments in these would-be states, there was little direct involvement on the part of Eastern suffragists. When it came to modifying the Colorado and Idaho state constitutions, Eastern suffrage organizers were on the scene to persuade individual voters to support the cause, but once the victory was realized the local organizations were difficult to maintain.

Further, Western suffragists were neither radical nor federalists; they usually persisted with a states' rights view. Generally, the spokesmen and Senators from the equal suffrage states held to their beliefs in the states' rights position on the subject. This was a convenient position for them because it kept the women back home content, but it did not put them in the uncomfortable political position of having to be woman suffrage advocates in Congress. Even in later years when the Nineteenth Amendment was under consideration, Western Senators, notably William E. Borah of Idaho, often opposed the federal suffrage amendment pleading states' rights. Borah, who had worked for woman suffrage in Idaho, said he believed in the accomplishment of woman suffrage through the individual action of states.

Thus, the year 1896 was important in that it seemed like a real beginning when two states allowed women to vote bringing the total to four. But the defeat of the referendum in California was far more symbolic of what lay ahead. The opposition had been rallied, and the state-by-state campaign program adopted by the suffragists would leave them exhausted. Further, the strongest political support suffragists had ever enjoyed dissolved when the Populist's party was swallowed by the larger Democratic party which generally had been hostile to women's participation in politics.

The Colorado campaign also had ushered in a new era in which suffragists moved more into the public arena. Whereas in the past they had petitioned legislatures and lobbied with congressmen, suffragists now spent more time with the public demonstrations designed to convert voters to their cause. Although the National American Woman Suffrage Association continued to pay lip service to the idea of a federal amendment, the idea was submerged as most of the organization's energy and time was spent on state campaigns, most of which were failures, until 1910 when success was realized in the state of Washington and the next year in California.

With these two victories some suffragists became convinced the suffrage bandwagon was rolling again. But other more militant suffragists like Harriett Stanton Blatch labeled these endless state campaigns "political crocheting" designed to

AK 1912

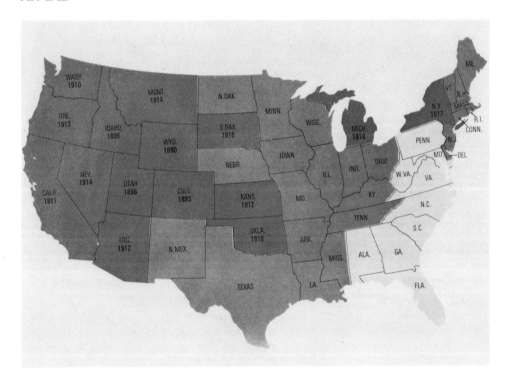

Dark shaded areas indicate equal woman suffrage state-wide and effective date
Medium shaded areas indicate partial woman suffrage
Light shaded areas indicate no state-wide woman suffrage

WOMAN SUFFRAGE BEFORE THE NINETEENTH AMENDMENT
Approval in 1920

keep the women busy and out of the way of the national legislators. In 1914 some of these militant women, who had adopted the more aggressive tactics used in England, bolted the National American Woman Suffrage Association and demanded passage of the Anthony amendment. These dissident feminists coalesced around Alice Paul, a young woman tutored in such dramatic tactics as were employed by the Pankhursts in England, to persuade the government to act on woman suffrage.

Faced by this new threat from within its own rank, the National American Woman Suffrage Association was revitalized when Carrie Chapman Catt took the presidency. She employed the organizing experience she had developed in the Colorado and Idaho campaigns to whip the association into a tightly organized, effective force, and she again focused its effort on passage of an amendment to the Constitution.

The fact that the woman suffrage movement was rejuvenated and once again sought the passage of a federal amendment, combined with the shift to the left of general American attitudes in the Progressive Era, resulted in passage of the Anthony amendment as the Nineteenth Amendment to the Constitution prohibiting the denial of the right to vote on the basis of sex.

Notes

[1]*History of Woman Suffrage*, 4:252.

[2]Janet Penrose Trevelyan, *The Life of Mrs. Humphry Ward* (New York: Dodd, Mead, 1923), pp. 225-28.

APPENDIX

NATIONAL AND STATE CONSTITUTION AMENDMENTS
AND LAWS RELATING TO WOMAN SUFFRAGE

The Fifteenth Amendment to the Constitution
of the United States

Article XV, Section 1. The right of citizens of the United States to vote shall not be denied or abridged by the United States or by any State on account of race, color or previous condition of servitude.

Section 2. The Congress shall have power to enforce this article by appropriate legislation.

Proposed February 27, 1869.
Declared Ratified March 30, 1870.

The Nineteenth Amendment to the Constitution
of the United States [also known as the Anthony
Amendment and a proposed Sixteenth Amendment]

Article XIX, Section 1. The right of citizens of the United States to vote shall not be denied or abridged by the United States or by any State on account of sex.

Section 2. The Congress shall have power, by appropriate legislation, to enforce the provisions of this article.

Proposed June 4, 1919.
Declared Ratified August 26, 1920.

An Act to Grant to the Women of Wyoming the
Right of Suffrage, and to Hold Office

Be it enacted by the Council and House of Representatives of the Territory of Wyoming:

Section 1. That every woman of the age of twenty-one years, residing in this Territory, may at every election to be holden under the law thereof, cast her vote. And her rights to the elective franchise and to hold office shall be the same under the election laws of the Territory, as those of electors.

Section 2. This act shall take effect and be in force from and after its passage.

Approved December 10, 1869.
Signed by Governor John A. Campbell.

An Act Conferring upon Women of Utah The Elective Franchise

Be it enabled by the Governor and Legislative Assembly of the Territory of Utah:

Section 1. That every woman of the age of twenty-one years who haʳ resided in this Territory six months next preceding any general or special election, born or naturalized citizen of the United States, shall be entitled to vote at any election in this Territory.

Section 2. All laws or parts of laws conflicting with this Act are hereby repealed.

Approved February 12, 1870.
Signed by Acting Governor S. A. Mann.

Woman Suffrage Bill Passed at the Ninth Session of the Colorado General Assembly

Section 1. That every female person shall be entitled to vote at all elections, in the same manner in all respects as male persons are, or shall be entitled to vote by the constitution and laws of this state, and the same qualifications as to age, citizenship, and the time of residence in the state, county, ward and precinct; and all other qualifications required by law to entitle male persons to vote shall be required to entitle female persons to vote.

Section 2. Section one of this act shall be submitted to the qualified voters of this state for approval at the general election in the present year 1893, and shall not be of effect as a law unless the same shall be approved by majority of the qualified electors voting thereon at said election.

Approved by the electorate of Colorado November, 1893.

Proposed Amendment to Idaho Constitution Submitted to the Electorate in 1896

Shall section 2, or article VI, of the constitution of the state of Idaho be so amended as to extend to women an equal right of suffrage?

Approved by the electorate of Idaho November, 1896.

BIBLIOGRAPHICAL NOTES

Manuscripts

Of central importance to any investigation of woman suffrage in the nineteenth century are the papers of the important leaders of the movement. The United States Library of Congress, Manuscript Division, Washington, D. C., has many letters written by and to Susan B. Anthony and Elizabeth Cady Stanton and a number of scrapbooks containing newspaper clippings concerning suffrage activities. In addition, handwritten copies of many of Stanton's speeches are deposited there, as are Anthony's diaries. The Manuscript Division also has over one hundred cartons of papers of Lucy Stone and Henry B. Blackwell.

The New York Public Library, New York City, holds the papers of a number of important national suffrage leaders, yet these letters and scrapbooks are more promising than rewarding on the subject of suffrage in the American West. The Susan B. Anthony Memorial, Inc., which is located in Anthony's former home in Rochester, New York, contains letters and photographs of women connected with the early suffrage work which were collected by Carrie Chapman Catt. The Sophia Smith Collection at the Smith College Library, Northampton, Massachusetts, contains numerous items on suffrage. While the Henry E. Huntington Library, San Marino, California, holds the papers of Ida H. Harper who compiled many histories on the suffrage movement and its leaders.

The Church Archives, Historical Department of the Church of Jesus Christ of Latter-day Saints, Salt Lake City, Utah, has an extensive collection of manuscripts concerning the Mormons and the West. The Journal History of the Church which consists of letters, reports, newspaper clippings, and extracts from the "History of Brigham Young" provides a chronological day-by-day account of events relating to the Mormons and Utah. Of the papers of officials and individuals in the Church Archives, the following were the most useful for this study: Wilford Woodruff, Emmeline B. Wells, and George Q. Cannon. The Utah State Historical Society, Salt Lake City, Utah, has a good collection of territorial documents including materials relating to the statehood efforts and the constitutional writing conventions. In addition, the diaries and letters of a number of Mormons and non-Mormons are located there. The papers of Abraham H. Cannon and John T. Caine were most rewarding for this study. Some materials are available at Brigham Young University Library Archives, Provo, Utah, on this subject. The Emmeline B. Wells diaries have recently been deposited at Brigham Young University Archives. The American West Collection of the Marriott Library of the University of Utah contains a number of important travel guides and rare books which were helpful. Documenting the activities of non-Mormons and ex-Mormons in Utah in the late nineteenth century is very difficult since their diaries and letter collections are almost impossible to locate. Thus, discussions with Hampton C. Godbe concerning his family's genealogy and history were helpful.

When it comes to studying the woman suffrage movement in Colorado and the impact that Colorado had as an example, the most useful sources are the newspaper and clipping files at the Colorado State Historical Society Library and the Western History Collection of the Denver Public Library, both of which are located in Denver, Colorado. Pertinent materials can be found in the Mary C. C. Bradford Manuscript Collection at the Colorado State Historical Society Library.

Background information on suffrage in Wyoming can be found in the Western History Center at the University of Wyoming, Laramie, and at the Wyoming State Archives and Historical Department of Cheyenne. The Idaho State Historical Society at Boise has the major collection of material for research on the Idaho woman suffrage campaigns. Abigail Scott Duniway's newspaper and her papers on file at the Oregon Historical Society provide supplemental materials for the Idaho story.

Newspapers and Periodical Literature

The late nineteenth century New York newspapers carried many articles about the woman suffrage movement; the *Times*, the *Herald*, and the *Tribune* (edited by Horace Greeley) are the most important. The two Denver newspapers, the *Rocky Mountain Herald* and the *Rocky Mountain News*, are the most useful sources of events in Colorado. For Wyoming, the most important newspapers are: the *Laramie Sentinel*, the *Cheyenne Leader*, and the *Wyoming Tribune*, a Republican paper published in Cheyenne by Territorial Secretary Edward M. Lee and his brother-in-law. The *Idaho Statesman* of Boise was a Republican newspaper edited by Milton Kelly and later by William Balderston, and the *Boise City Republican* was a prosuffrage, anti-Mormon newspaper, while the *Idaho Democrat* was a pro-Mormon paper published in Montpelier. Abigail Scott Duniway's *New Northwest*, published in Portland, Oregon, contains many articles on events in Idaho in addition to national suffrage activities. A comparative analysis of the discussion of events as reported in the Mormon newspaper, the *Deseret News*, and the *Salt Lake Tribune*, which mirrored the non-Mormon opionion is most useful. The *Herald* of Salt Lake City, which usually expressed a pro-Mormon, Democratic point of view, is also helpful. Jennie Anderson Froiseth's *Anti-Polygamy Standard*, published in Salt Lake City gives an impression of the non-Mormons' feelings; while the *Woman's Exponent* edited by Emmeline B. Wells represents the Mormon point of view. *The Latter-Day Saints' Millennial Star*, Liverpool, England, has newspaper clippings and letters from Church authorities describing events in Utah and the West. While *Tullidge Quarterly Magazine* and the *Utah Magazine*, edited by E. L. T. Harrison and Edward W. Tullidge, expressed a liberal Morman view and recorded some of the earliest statements on women's rights in Utah.

Movement newspapers and magazines provide an excellent source of the writings of leaders of the woman suffrage movement. Moreover, they reflect the changing concerns and arguments put forth by the feminists. The *Revolution* (New York, 1868-72), edited by Susan B. Anthony and Elizabeth Cady Stanton and initially financed by George Francis Train, was the first important suffrage newspaper. Emily Pitts Stevens published the *Pioneer* in San Francisco, and Clara B. Colby edited her *Woman's Tribune* in Beatrice, Nebraska. *Queen Bee* edited in Denver, Colorado, by Mrs. C. M. Churchill, whose masthead declared that it was "the only paper in the state advocating woman's political equality and individuality," was a strong voice for woman suffrage. The *Woman's Journal*, edited by Mary A. Livermore, Julia Ward Howe, Lucy Stone, William Lloyd Garrison, and T. W. Higginson, reflected the more conservative view of the Boston-centered group that organized the American Woman Suffrage Association. A more radical feminist point of view was voiced in *Woodhull and Claflin's Weekly* (New York, 1870-1876) edited by Victoria Woodhull and Tennessee Claflin.

Nonfeminist magazines also published many articles concerning woman suffrage. The most useful are: *Godey's Magazine and Lady's Book; Harper's Weekly; Arena;* the *Atlantic Monthly;* and *Outlook.* There were also a number of journals expressing a position in opposition to woman suffrage. *Kate Field's Washington,* a weekly review edited by Kate Field, expressed an anti-Mormon point of view and was not a strong supporter of the woman suffrage until after 1893. There were also a number of antisuffrage magazines: *True Woman* (Baltimore and Washington, 1870-73) edited monthly by Mrs. Charlotte E. McKay and the English antisuffrage *Nineteenth Century Magazine.*

General Works on Woman Suffrage
in the American West

T. A. Larson of the University of Wyoming has published the most detailed articles on woman suffrage in the American West. His presidential address to the 1971 Western History Association Convention which was published in *The Western Historical Quarterly* 3 (January 1972):55-16, is his best survey of woman suffrage in the West. The most detailed and thoroughly documented version of this speech and article is "Emancipating the West's Dolls, Vassals and Hopeless Drudges: The Origins of Woman Suffrage in the West," in Roger Daniels, ed., *Essays in Western History in Honor of T. A. Larson,* University of Wyoming Publications, Volume 37 (Laramie 1971). Larson puts the enfranchisement of the women of Wyoming into context in his chapter on the organization of Wyoming territory and adoption of woman suffrage in his *History of Wyoming* (Lincoln: University of Nebraska Press, 1965), pp. 64-94. In addition, he has published a number of articles dealing with woman suffrage in specific states or territories: "Petticoats at the Polls: Woman Suffrage in Territorial Wyoming," *Pacific Northwest Quarterly* 44 (April 1953):74-79; "Woman Suffrage in Western America," *Utah Historical Quarterly* 38 (Winter 1970):7-19; 'Woman's Right's in Idaho," *Idaho Yesterdays* 16 (Spring 1972):2-15, 18-19; "Montana Woman and the Battle for the Ballot," *Montana, The Magazine of Western History* 23 (Winter 1973):24-41. By examining the social, economic, and political background of the members of the territorial and state legislatures which passed legislation enabling women to vote, Larson attempts to discover motives. This method was especially revealing of the state of affairs in Wyoming when the woman suffrage bill was first passed.

In addition to Larson's studies on Wyoming, there is Miriam Gantz Chapman's "The Story of Woman Suffrage in Wyoming, 1869-1890," an unpublished master's thesis, University of Wyoming, 1952. In 1890 Hamilton Willcox published an authoritative account of how women were enfranchised in Wyoming entitled: "Wyoming: The True Cause and Splendid Fruits of Woman Suffrage There from Official Records and Personal Knowledge correcting the errors of Horace Plunkett and Professor Bryce and supplying omissions in the *History of Woman Suffrage* by Mrs. Stanton, Mrs. Gage, and Miss Anthony, and in the *History of Wyoming* by Hubert Howe Bancroft with other information about the state" (New York: November 1890), 28 pages. This valuable pamphlet is available at the Bancroft Library, Berkeley, California.

In his article "An Experiment in Progressive Legislation: The Granting of Woman Suffrage in Utah in 1870," *Utah Historical Quarterly* 38 (Winter 1970):20-30, Thomas G. Alexander argues that the Mormons were progressive, ahead of their time, in supporting woman suffrage. Susa Young Gates brought together most of the information on woman suffrage in Utah which found its way into most official histories of the suffrage movement in the United States. Additional information can be found by examining her miscellaneous file in the Widtsoe Collection at the Utah State Historical Society. Gates' greatest fault was that she completely ignored non-Mormon involvement in the suffrage movement. In 1944 in the fifth volume of the Daughters of Utah Pioneers publication, *Heart Throbs of the West*, Kate B. Carter compiled selections from newspapers, histories, and summary accounts, especially those of Susa Young Gates, on woman suffrage in the West. While Ralph Lorenzo Jack's "Woman Suffrage in Utah as an Issue in the Mormon and Non-Mormon Press of the Territory, 1870-1887," a master's thesis submitted at Brigham Young University in 1954, does not attempt to analyze the woman suffrage activities in detail, the study does demonstrate how the two sides used the idea of woman suffrage to promote their cause. In her February 14, 1974, Charles Redd Lecture at Brigham Young University, Jean Bickmore White detailed the events surrounding the inclusion of woman suffrage in the 1895 constitution. This lecture has been printed as a Redd Series monograph and as an article in the *Utah Historical Quarterly* 42 (Fall 1974):344-69.

While T. A. Larson's studies of Wyoming and Idaho are the most detailed ones available, Billie Barnes Jensen's 1959 Master's thesis in history at the University of Colorado is the most thorough presentation of the facts concerning the woman suffrage movement in Colorado. Later, she presented her findings in two articles: "Let the Women Vote," *Colorado Magazine* 41 (Winter 1964):13-25 and "Colorado Woman Suffrage Campaigns of the 1870's," *Journal of the West* 12 (April 1973):254-71.

Endorsed by the Non-Partisan Colorado Equal Suffrage Association, Joseph G. Brown's *History of Equal Suffrage in Colorado, 1869-1898*, published in Denver in 1898 by the News Job Printing Company, still stands as a fine review of the story; however, like most endorsed studies, it gives extensive lists of personalities involved in the suffrage campaign. An interesting analysis was published in the July 1956 *Colorado Magazine* in which William B. Faherty examined "Regional Minorities and the Woman Suffrage Struggle." In this study he revealed some of the racist overtones of the suffrage debate in Colorado.

In *The Puritan Ethic and Woman Suffrage* (New York: Oxford, 1967), which deals primarily with woman suffrage in the West, Alan P. Grimes, employing status anxiety techniques similar to those developed by Richard Hostader, argues that "the constituency granting woman suffrage was composed of those who also supported prohibition and immigration restriction and felt woman suffrage would further their enactment." Grimes errs in his analysis in that he reads backwards into history. The issues of prohibition and immigration restriction were not very important in 1869-1871 when the subject of woman suffrage was first introduced in the four intermountain areas of Wyoming, Utah, Colorado, and Idaho. They became important issues at a later date. Sandra L. Myres provides an excellent chapter on western women and the struggle for political, legal and economic rights in *Westering Women and the Frontier Experience 1800-1915* (Albuquerque: University of New Mexico Press, 1982).

General Works on Woman Suffrage

The single most comprehensive and basic source of original material on the woman suffrage movement in the United States is the six-volume *History of Woman Suffrage* edited by Elizabeth Cady Stanton, Susan B. Anthony, Maltilda J. Gage, and Ida H. Haper originally published 1881-1922 (reprint edition, New York: Arno, 1969). An analysis entitled *Woman Suffrage and Politics: The Inner Story of the Suffrage Movement* by Carrie Chapman Catt and Nettie Rogers Shuler was published in 1923; it has been reprinted with an introduction by T. A. Larson (Seattle: University of Washington, 1969). Pauline W. Davis' small volume, *A History of the National Women's Rights Movement* (New York: Journeymen Printers Co-operative Association, 1871, reprinted by Source Book Press, 1970), is a good source of details for woman suffrage for the years, 1870-1871. The best interpretive studies of woman suffrage are Eleanor Flexner's *Century of Struggle: the Woman's Rights Movement in the United States* (Cambridge: Harvard, 1958) which is an institutional study; Aileen Karditor's ideological study *The Ideas of the Woman Suffrage Movement, 1890-1920* (New York: Columbia, 1965); and Ellen C. DuBois' *Feminism and Suffrage: The Emergence of an Independent Woman's Movement in America, 1848-1869* (Ithaca: Cornell University Press, 1978).

Autobiographies and biographies of prominent leaders provide some first-hand impressions of events that influenced the suffrage movement, but since they are usually designed to give a favorable picture of the subject, they should be used with care. What is omitted from these studies is sometimes more important than what is included. The most colorful account is Abigail Scott Duniway's *Path Breaking: An Autobiographical History of the Equal Suffrage Movement in Pacific Coast States* (Portland, Oregon: James, Kerns, and Abbott, 1914) which includes a view of activities in Idaho. Alma Lutz's *Susan B. Anthony: Rebel, Crusader, Humanitarian* (Boston: Beacon, 1959) and Katherine Anthony's *Susan B. Anthony: Her Personal History and Her Era* (New York: Doubleday, 1954) provide some insight into the world of this energetic suffrage leader. Alma Lutz has written a number of books dealing with the women's rights movement including an individual biographical study of Elizabeth Cady Stanton entitled *Created Equal* (New York: John Day, 1940). Stanton put down her reminiscences in *Eighty Years and More* (New York: European Publishing, 1898). Though it deals primarily with her personal life and her career as a preacher, Anna Howard Shaw's autobiography, *The Story of a Pioneer* (New York: Harper, 1915), does provide some information about the suffrage movement. The Radcliffe College sponsored three-volume biographical dictionary, *Notable American Women, 1607-1950* (Cambridge: Harvard University Press, 1971), edited by Edward T. James, provides the most accurate and useful sketches of women of national prominence. In his study, *American Feminists* (Lawrence, Kansas, 1963), in which he tries to analyze the motivating forces behind feminists, Robert E. Riegel provides a number of sketches of leaders of the suffrage movement.

General histories which provide background information and give some account of the woman suffrage movement are: Page Smith's *Daughters of the Promised Land: Women in American History* (Boston: Little, Brown, 1970) though he does not mention Utah; Mary R. Beard's *America Through Women's Eyes* (New York: Macmillan, 1933) and *Woman as Force in History* (New York: Macmillan, 1946). William L. O'Neill's *Everyone Was Brave: The Rise and Fall of Feminism in America* (Chicago: Quadrangle, 1969) has a section on suffrage in which he describes the two generations of suffragists and their attitudes. Trevor Lloyd's *Suffragettes International: The World-Wide Campaign for Women's Rights* (New York: American Heritage Press, 1971) is an excellent collection of illustrations and photographs; however, the text contains numerous factual errors. In *Women's Suffrage and Prohibition: A Comparative Study of Equality and Social Control* (Glenview, Illinois: Scott-Foresman, 1973), Ross Evans Paulson does a fine job of showing the interrelationship between these two movements in his international comparative study.